Haunted
Places
of
Kent

Rupert Matthews

COUNTRYSIDE BOOKS
NEWBURY BERKSHIRE

First published 2004
© Rupert Matthews 2004

COUNTRYSIDE BOOKS
3 Catherine Road
Newbury, Berkshire

To view our complete range of books,
please visit us at
www.countrysidebooks.co.uk

ISBN 1 85306 865 9

Cover painting supplied by Anthony Wallis

Designed by Peter Davies, Nautilus Design

Produced through MRM Associates Ltd., Reading
Printed by Cromwell Press, Trowbridge

· Contents ·

HAUNTED PLACES OF KENT

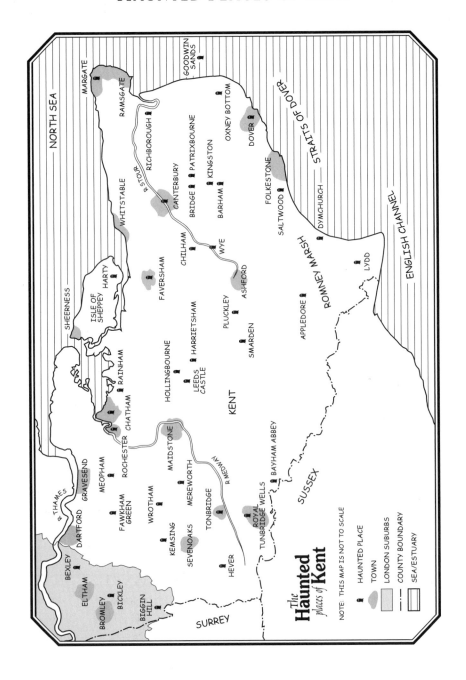

The
Haunted
places of **Kent**

NOTE: THIS MAP IS NOT TO SCALE

- HAUNTED PLACE
- TOWN
- LONDON SUBURBS
- COUNTY BOUNDARY
- SEA/ESTUARY

• Introduction •

For centuries, the county of Kent has been known as the Garden of England – and with good reason. The fruits and hops grown here have been recognised for generations as being among the best, not just in England, but in Europe.

Travelling around Kent to research this book, talking to those who have seen the ghosts and photographing the haunted places themselves has been a wonderful experience. Although many supermarkets prefer to import cheaper fruits from abroad, the Kent orchards still produce their magnificent fruits, which can be bought at the roadside or in local shops.

Kent, though, is not just the Garden of England, but also its gateway. These days the railway and M20 carry holidaymakers and travellers to the Channel Tunnel and the Channel ports. In the past it was stagecoaches and shanks's pony that did duty. Most visitors to and from the continent used to come through Kent. Not all of them were peaceful. Celts, Romans, Saxons and Vikings all came this way into Britain, and it was here that the natives fought to keep them out.

Such stirring historic events cost the lives of thousands of men, and their ghosts still walk the fields and lanes of Kent. A Celtic chariot races down the hill at Bridge, Romans march at Richborough and a Saxon warrior fights eternally in spectral form at Kits Coty, just south of Chatham. Nor are these the only invaders to leave a spectral mark on the county. A Luftwaffe bomber of the Second World War continues to re-enact its last fatal seconds over Romney Marsh, while one of the defending RAF Spitfires is seen occasionally over the wartime air base at Biggin Hill.

Of course, Kent has not been all war and bloodshed. Many of her ghosts date from more peaceful times when rural life here pottered along in its everyday way and these ghosts are perfectly inoffensive spirits. Ladies walk quietly in churchyards and men amble down country lanes. They are as gentle and unassuming in spectral form as they were in human form. They trot about the county on whatever business it is that they have here, disturbing nobody and wanting nothing more than to be left alone to get on with their tasks.

Some people may object that there are no such things as ghosts, but that cannot be true in Kent. In the course of researching this book, I met many people who have seen the phantoms, or heard them, and know very well what it was that they experienced.

Just what ghosts may be, on a scientific or philosophical level, neither these witnesses nor I pretend to know. We are convinced, though, that ghosts do walk and that they are abroad in this lovely county of Kent.

Rupert Matthews

· The West ·

BICKLEY

The Chequers Inn in Southborough Lane, Bickley, is one of those places which seems to be a positive magnet for our ghostly companions.

The most notorious of the Bickley phantoms is the young gentleman in green velvet who sits quietly in a corner of the bar. Those who have seen the phantom describe him as having dark hair, covered by a large hat decorated with an extravagant plumed feather. The clothes of this man place him firmly in the 18th century and local legend names him as none other than Dick Turpin.

This most famous of highwaymen was known to visit the Chequers when lying low after a profitable crime. The layout of the pub with convenient back stairs and more than one exit enabled Turpin to make a quick getaway if necessary. The image of Dick Turpin that has been cultivated over the years is a glamorous one. Riding his magnificent charger Black Bess, Turpin is dressed in fine clothes and is unfailingly courteous to those he robs. In many stories, Turpin takes on corrupt local officials to the benefit of honest farmers and pretty girls.

It is an image which was assiduously promoted by the highwaymen themselves. For instance, Jack Rann made a point of spending his ill-gotten gains on clothes. When he was eventually arrested in September 1774, Rann ordered a new suit for his trial. He appeared in pea-green wool, lined with blue satin and edged with silver lace. He even went to the trouble of ordering a new and ostentatiously flamboyant hat to wear at his public execution. Another outlaw, James Maclean, was tall and handsome. He chose to spend his money buying jewels and treats for an apparently endless succession of young ladies whom he attempted to seduce with varying degrees of success. At his trial in 1750 several ladies of quality came forward as character witnesses, but he was hanged anyway.

Turpin, however, was no such dashing gentleman. Born in Essex in 1705, Turpin took to poaching as a teenager. He soon graduated to burglary, rape and torture. In 1735 Turpin took to the road. He held up coaches, shot drivers and mercilessly beat up those who resisted him. He even shot his own partner. By all accounts, Turpin was a violent, vicious crook with none of the panache associated with men such as Rann or Maclean. He was, however, hugely successful and netted a fortune from his crimes. Typically, Turpin committed his misdeeds north of the Thames, and went into hiding south of the river. In 1738 Turpin left the countryside around London as the authorities cracked down on street crime. He went to Yorkshire, but the forces of law and order

The Chequers Inn, Southborough Lane, Bickley, is haunted by a gentleman who many believe to be none other than Dick Turpin, the famous highwayman.

were even more diligent there. Turpin was arrested for horse stealing, recognised for who he was and hanged.

Why Turpin became transformed into a hero, while other highwaymen were forgotten is unclear. But if he is the ghost in the Chequers, then he is acting true to form. He keeps himself to himself, which is just what Turpin did when he came here to avoid the law.

The other resident ghost at the Chequers is a very busy lady who haunts the upstairs rooms. She seems to date back to about the same time as Turpin, but whether the two are linked in any way is unknown. She walks around the upper floor with determined and hurried steps. Most often only the sound of her footsteps alerts listeners to the fact that she is about. Trotting up the stairs, bustling along the corridor, padding into bedrooms, her footsteps might be heard anywhere. This ghost also slams doors. Any left open are liable to be closed loudly as the footsteps pass by. Only occasionally is the lady actually seen. Even then she is busy. She is glimpsed fleetingly, usually as she hurries past a doorway or nips in and out of a room at speed.

Why she should be so busy is a mystery. Most visitors to the Chequers prefer to linger over a drink or one of the landlord's finely cooked meals.

BEXLEY

'You have come to the right place for ghosties', announced Annie of the Bexley Heritage Trust which now runs Hall Place. And she is right because Hall Place has three phantoms.

Now open to the public, Hall Place was for many years an educational centre run by the local council. The house has since been renovated and restored and offers well-tended gardens, with a gift shop and restaurant, as well as a fascinating house to attract visitors.

The most famous of the ghosts is that of the Black Prince. So well known is this phantom that the pub just outside the grounds of Hall Place is named after him, though it does not go so far as to offer any stuffed boar's heads or other medieval delicacies to welcome the long-dead warrior!

HAUNTED PLACES OF KENT

Hall Place in Bexley has several ghosts which are seen with some regularity.

The Black Prince was more properly known as Prince Edward, eldest son of King Edward III and he was one of the greatest warriors of Christendom. Edward stayed at Hall Place for some time in the spring of 1346 while the king and his advisers prepared the expeditionary force which would invade France that summer.

The campaign culminated on 26th August in the Battle of Crécy. The English army, some 9,000 strong, was caught by a French army of over 30,000 men. In the ensuing battle the English proved that their longbows and halberds were superior to the French swords and inflicted enormous losses. It is thought that the French lost 11 royal princes, 1,200 knights and 10,000 men at arms killed or captured in the fighting. The English lost barely a thousand men. At one point in the battle young Prince Edward's division looked likely to be overwhelmed by a French attack. Noblemen begged King Edward to send his son reinforcements, but the king refused saying merely 'Suffer him to win his spurs this day'.

Prince Edward obviously liked Hall Place for he returned there more than once between his frequent campaigns and battles. Indeed he married a local noble lady, Joan, whose beauty was so famous that she became known as 'The Fair Maid of Kent'.

The need to fight wars to protect England kept Edward abroad for months on end but at the age of just 40 he was struck down by a disease which kept him invalided and in pain for over five years, until his death in 1376. It might be thought that it is to recapture the gentle, peaceful days of courtship that the phantom of the Black Prince returns to Hall Place. It would appear not, however, for when the Black Prince walks the gardens of this magnificent estate, he does so in his armour.

And this warlike appearance matches his purpose. The ghost walks only when either the owners of Hall Place or England itself are in some danger.

In the early 20th century the property was owned by Lady Limerick, and during this period the ghost was seen four times. On each occasion a family death occurred soon after. In 1940 he was seen just two days before the German panzer attack that led to the British retreat that ended at Dunkirk. Fortunately, perhaps, he has not been seen in recent years.

Rather more active is the sad phantom of Lady Constance Hall. Not that one should normally discuss a lady's age, but this is one of the older ghosts of Kent, though not the oldest (see Dover). Lady Constance is considerably older than the Black Prince, having lived here in the 13th century.

The story of Lady Constance is not a happy one. On a bright summer's afternoon her husband, Sir Thomas Hall, was returning from a day's hunting in the woodland that in those days surrounded this fine building. Sir Thomas had had a good day with his friends and bagged a variety of fine animals for the table, and the trophy wall. He was particularly proud of a large stag which boasted a magnificent spread of antlers. Unfortunately for Sir Thomas, the stag was unconscious but not dead. When he arrived home, he triumphantly threw the large stag from the pack horse on which it had travelled to lie on the stones. This awoke the stag which, enraged by its pain, turned on Sir Henry and gored him to death. Lady Constance witnessed this horrific incident.

A few days later, driven mad by grief, she hurled herself to her death from a tower. From that day to this the pale ghost of Lady Constance has wandered

Hall Place wailing and weeping. It is a most upsetting ghost to encounter, as staff here will tell you.

The third ghost of Hall Place is, by comparison, of a rather less illustrious person. This is a helpful young woman who flits about one of the upstairs bedrooms. She is the ghost of a servant girl who died here over a century ago. She did not die after an unhappy love affair, nor did she achieve fame in her life. She is just an ordinary servant girl who returns to visit the rooms for which she once cared.

The final evidence for the existence of these ghosts comes from Annie, who says 'The house is definitely haunted. According to various members of staff the white lady wears grey and has been seen through the corner of the eye and felt running past staff within the house at the bottom of the tower. The stairs of this tower were removed some time ago - the story goes that this was a former inhabitant's attempt to stop the ghost from walking. It obviously didn't work. Other staff members have also felt strange vibrations in the Great Hall floor as if someone was walking around but no one was there.'

FAWKHAM GREEN

Fawkham Green is one of those charmingly quaint villages that manage to survive just outside the M25 where the sprawl of London housing estates has not yet reached. Of course, there are commuters here and, on occasion, the roar of engines from nearby Brands Hatch motor racing circuit can disturb the calm, but on the whole it is a quiet place.

Five centuries ago, this quiet little village was the scene of a quite horrific crime. It was a crime which has resulted in the restless wandering of a ghost, even to this day. A gang of footpads were making their way through the village towards a main road where they hoped to find a rich prize. In Pennis Lane they came across a lone nun, peacefully walking towards Canterbury.

The toughs waylaid the nun, perhaps in the hope of finding a valuable golden crucifix or other treasure of the church on her but the poor woman had none, being one of the few religious of the time who kept their vows of poverty. Disappointed in their search for plunder, the robbers turned to violence and then to rape. The nun's screams and yells reached the ears of a pair of local gentlemen who came galloping to her rescue. They drove off the robbers, and carried the battered woman to nearby Pennis House but to little avail. The nun was too badly injured and died a few days later.

But, before she died the nun blessed those who had rescued her. She promised that if her skull was kept in Pennis House then good fortune and prosperity would come to the owners. But if her skull was ever removed then bad luck and adversity would surely follow. In consequence of these somewhat bizarre final words, the owners of Pennis House duly had the nun buried without her head and kept the severed skull in their house.

The lonely Pennis Lane in Fawkham Green is the haunt of a nun murdered here many centuries ago.

Only once, in the mid-19th century, has the skull not rested there. The then owner did not hold with medieval superstition. He was a rational Victorian scientist and believed only in solid facts. He had the skull taken away and buried in the churchyard.

A few days later it became clear that there was an intruder in the house. Or so the scientist thought. Doors were slammed shut. Doors were thrown open. Objects were moved. Then the muttering began. It was like a human voice, but faint as if heard through a shut door. No matter where the scientist and his staff looked, they could find nobody who could be causing the disturbances. The house was searched from cellar to attic and back again. There was nobody there, but still the doors opened and closed, objects moved and a faint muttering was heard. In the end the poor owner gave in. The skull was unearthed and brought back to Pennis House. Peace returned.

Not so the tranquillity of Pennis Lane. Several times a year, as dusk begins to fall, the nun walks again. She floats along with no sign of her feet moving beneath her robes. Suddenly she stops, turns and begins to run. Clearly frightened, the nun seems to be screaming, but no sounds are heard. Then, suddenly and abruptly, she vanishes. Finally the sound of pounding hooves comes thundering down the lane to the spot where the nun has just vanished, where they stop just as abruptly. Presumably the ghosts are replaying the fatal events of that summer's evening five hundred years ago.

MEOPHAM

Meopham lies astride the main road running from Gravesend to Tonbridge, and a busy little village it is too. Busy with ghosts, that is. So busy, in fact, that this village found itself the centre of a scientific investigation of the paranormal which was broadcast, live, on BBC radio in 1936. The investigation was carried out by Harry Price, then the most famous ghost hunter in Europe. Price was a serious investigator of odd events and happenings who contributed much to early studies of the paranormal. Unfortunately he was later found to have considerably embellished some of his accounts in order to gain publicity. As a result, his records have tended to be discounted.

His work at Meopham, however, was witnessed by independent observers and broadcast live, so he had little chance to exaggerate what went on.

Price visited Meopham because of the tale of a phantom servant girl in the cellar of Dean Manor. While on air, the thermometer measuring the air temperature suddenly plummeted several degrees, a phenomenon which many people who see a ghost, or experience its presence, remark on. In addition to the sudden chill in the air, Price also recorded the faint sound of footsteps, as if

A man in a great cloak walks from the pub to this church in Meopham.

coming from upstairs. Dean Manor is now a private house and is not open to the public.

Fortunately, however, there is more than one ghost at Meopham. The most active is the headless man in a long cloak who is seen walking toward the church. Local stories say this man is a monk, but the descriptions of him do not really bear this out. His attire sounds more like that of a coachman of the 19th century than of a monk of the Middle Ages. Whoever this ghost might be, he appears near to the pub, before heading down the road towards the church. He walks between two pillars and then fades from view. Unlike some ghosts he does not vanish abruptly, but is said gently to become fainter until he is gone entirely.

The final ghost of Meopham lurks in Steeles Lane. She is a startlingly attractive young lady dressed in orange silk. This is Mademoiselle Pinard from Paris and her story is a sad, but familiar one.

In the aftermath of the defeat of the French Emperor Napoleon at the Battle of Waterloo in 1815, the British army was sent to occupy Paris. Its task was to keep order while the re-established regime of King Louis XVIII was installed. In the event, the French caused little trouble and the British army did not have much to do. One soldier in Paris was a private in the Buffs, Kent's premier regiment. With time on his hands the young man dallied with Mlle Pinard, promising to marry her in due course. As a result, the pretty young Parisienne surrendered to the soldier rather more of her virtue than was normal in those days.

Of course, the regiment eventually left Paris and was sent home to Kent. Believing her lover's promises, Mlle Pinard scraped together enough money to buy a wedding dress and to pay for her fare to Kent. Arriving in Meopham at the soldier's home, the girl found herself cold shouldered by the man who no longer had any need for her charms. Distraught and penniless, Mlle Pinard dressed herself in what was supposed to be her wedding dress and hanged

---

Steeles Lane in Meopham is the haunt of Kent's most beautiful ghost,
though the darkly attractive lady has a tragic history.

herself in Steeles Lane. Her ghost lurks there still, standing quietly by the side of the road on the spot where she died. Hers was a sad death, but served as a warning. In the 19th century many mothers in Kent would point to the sad phantom and admonish their daughters to get their man up the aisle before surrendering to him.

ROCHESTER

The town of Rochester is dominated by a royal castle and a cathedral, huge stone manifestations of the twin powers in medieval England, the crown and the church. Both these edifices are haunted, but by very different phantoms.

The ghost of Rochester Castle appears only in the spring. She is a beautiful lady dressed in a flowing white gown and with long black hair. A patch of red blood stains her chest. This is the ghost of the beautiful Lady Blanche de Warrenne who was killed by an arrow during the 1264 siege of Rochester Castle. The castle was held by men loyal to King Henry III, while the attackers were the army of Simon de Montfort, Earl of Leicester, who wanted the king to pay more attention to the views of his subjects.

A romantic legend has grown up around this ghost, though how true it might be is hard to tell. One of the knights in the castle was Sir Ralph de Capo, who was betrothed to Lady Blanche. Among the attackers was Sir Gilbert de Clare, a brave enough knight but a man with a violent temper. Only months before Lady Blanche had broken off her engagement to de Clare in favour of an alliance with de Capo.

After the siege had lasted some weeks, Montfort learned that King Henry was at Lewes with a small force. He called off the siege and marched off to Lewes where he captured the king and enforced his own demands for better government. As the rebel army marched off, de Capo came out to harass stragglers and chase off looters. Sir Gilbert saw his chance, and slipped into the virtually undefended castle. He found Lady Blanche on the battlements anxiously awaiting the return of her beloved. Realising Clare could not have

The tallest turret of Rochester Castle is haunted by a lady in white who met a sad death here over 600 years ago.

honourable motives, Blanche fled to the round tower at one corner of the keep. The knight was undeterred, however, and battered down the door, reaching Lady Blanche at the uppermost part of the castle.

At this point de Capo returned from his foray and saw his betrothed struggling with his rival. Grabbing a bow, de Capo sent an arrow winging upwards. He was a famed archer and the arrow struck Clare on the chest. Unfortunately, it glanced off his armour and plunged into Lady Blanche's chest. She died instantly.

It is a romantic tale and fits the bloody history of the castle well.

The ghost at the cathedral is slightly less romantic. The gentle old man who potters about the graveyard near the west door of the cathedral is Charles Dickens. The great novelist lived in Kent from the age of four. Although the family later moved to London, Dickens returned to Kent as soon as he could afford to purchase the house at Gads Hill, which he had coveted as a boy. In his later years, Dickens was a familiar figure in Rochester. He loved the cathedral there and asked to be buried near the west door in a spot that had once been the castle moat. But when Dickens died, his remains were taken to Westminster Abbey to grace Poet's Corner. His ghost, however, remained in Rochester. It is said the phantom, seen only in the evenings, moves slowly around the tombs reading the inscriptions. Perhaps he is looking endlessly for his own monument, which sadly is not there.

Dickens has also been seen outside the Corn Exchange. He appears there in broad daylight to check his pocket watch against the clock on the wall, then turns to walk off towards the cathedral. He can appear at any time and seems to be very solid and natural. No doubt several people have seen this ghost and not realised that they were looking at anything more unusual than an elderly man in old-fashioned clothes.

As this plaque records, the novelist Charles Dickens wished to be buried here beside Rochester Cathedral, but a grateful nation had him interred at Westminster Abbey instead. Now his ghost returns, perhaps looking for his grave.

The Cooper's Arms in St Margaret Street is perhaps the oldest secular building in Rochester. It was once a workshop for the priory, which is no longer there. It was here, as the name suggests, that the priors' barrels were made and it is the ghost of one of those long-dead holy men that returns to the Cooper's Arms. He walks out of the wall of the bar quite suddenly and dramatically. Having had a good look around the bar, he vanishes as if he had never been there. This is a most startling phantom, but he is usually seen only in the autumn and rarely more than once or twice each year.

The George Inn also has a ghost in its bar. This particular ghost is most convivial. He is a little old man who seems forever trying to catch somebody's eye. He bobs about and smiles, winking when he gets a person to look at him, rather like one of Dickens's colourful characters. He then slowly fades from sight but who he is and what he wants is a mystery.

So far the ghosts of Rochester have been relatively normal – if ghosts can be said to be normal. But the things that lurk at Blue Bell Hill are anything but

The Cooper's Arms in Rochester once formed part of the long-vanished priory.

conventional. Several motorists have been scared by something as they drive past the woods of Blue Bell Hill. Thinking they may have run down a valuable creature, perhaps escaped from a zoo, they have reported the incident to the police. The creature is variously said to be a gorilla, a leopard, a bear and a lion. Whatever it is, it is big and hairy and not the sort of creature you would want to encounter on your own.

CHATHAM

Chatham has been a naval and military town for centuries, therefore it would be natural to assume that any phantom in uniform seen here must be that of a naval or army man. But our first phantom is neither of these.

The 'Man in Green' does, however, wear a smart uniform with peaked cap and metal buttons. He lurks inside an old hall in the High Street, and seems quite friendly. The ghost was first seen in the 1970s when cleaners working upstairs after the public had gone home would catch a glimpse of a figure walking out of sight round a corner or through a doorway. Only after several of the staff had chased the figure to find themselves alone did they realise that a ghost might be at work.

When a psychic visited the hall she produced the name Bill Malan. Retired staff were contacted and it was found that there had, indeed, been a commissionaire named William Malan in the 1930s and 1940s when the building had been a cinema. Moreover, the commissionaire's uniform was a smart coat of dark green and matching trousers. Malan had been on duty one terrible night in the autumn of 1940 when German bombers came over as part of the Blitz which pounded so much of London to rubble. Families whose homes had been bombed in earlier raids were given temporary shelter in the cinema. This night a bomb fell on the cinema, burying many of the homeless in the wreckage. Malan worked with others to clear the destruction and, like them, was distraught to find three children among the dead. Perhaps this incident accounts for the sounds of children's voices that have also sometimes been heard in this building.

A few doors down from the hall, now used for bingo, is No.122 High Street. This shop has long been the site of a haunting by a young woman who is seen standing downstairs brushing her hair. More than one shop assistant has mistaken her for a customer and approached her, only to find the figure suddenly vanishes. This ghost was particularly active in the 1960s, when the shop was a lady's boutique named Snob. On one occasion she was seen upstairs, though the sales floor is very much her preferred home.

There are, however, military ghosts in Chatham. The more enigmatic of the two manifests itself at St Mary's Barracks. In the middle watch, that is between midnight and 4 am, limping footsteps approach the entrance to St Mary's Barracks. Known as Peg Leg Jack, this ghost is never seen but his footsteps are heard fairly regularly. They have also been reported near the Cumberland Block. It is assumed he is a wounded ex-sailor returning to his barrack block long after he last lived here.

Kits Coty, just outside Chatham, is the scene for a spectral battle between two long dead warriors.

More famous is the ghost which is seen striding purposefully around the dockyards. This is Admiral Nelson, the heroic commander who won a series of spectacular naval victories for Britain and became the nation's hero. Nelson is best known for his last victory, that of Trafalgar in 1805. With a fleet of 27 ships, Nelson tackled a combined French and Spanish fleet of 33 ships, for the most part larger than their British opponents. The fighting lasted most of the day and ended with 20 ships having surrendered to Nelson and the rest so badly damaged as to be useless. Nelson was shot by a sniper at the height of the battle and died that night. This was Nelson's last and greatest victory and it gave Britain control of the seas for over a century.

Interestingly the ghost that is seen at Chatham is that of a youthful Nelson, before he lost his arm and an eye in battles against the French. Why this should be is unknown. And given the determined way in which this ghost marches about, it is unlikely anyone is going to stop him and ask questions.

More ghosts with a military background can be encountered south of the town beside the A229. In a small fenced enclosure stand three large upright stones, which are known as Kits Coty House. They are all that remain of a once much larger burial mound constructed around 2,500 BC. About 400 yards away a tumbled collection of boulders may be the ruins of another ancient tomb. It is between these two burial sites that the ghosts are seen.

One of the warriors at Kits Coty is believed to be Horsa, leader of the first English invaders to land in Roman Britain around the year 450.

The phantoms are two tall, muscular warriors who are forever fighting each other. Equipped with spears and round shields these two men seem so deeply engrossed in their struggle that they pay no attention to anything around them. The endless battle never reaches a decision for the phantoms disappear before either of them beats the other.

One local story maintains that the men date from the 5th century when the Germanic mercenaries hired by the local Britons rebelled to take over the country. Inviting thousands of fellow warriors over from Germany, the newcomers established a new nation - the English. The earliest leaders of the new nation were two brothers, Hengest and Horsa. It is said that the battling phantoms are Horsa and the local British governor who fought a single combat to decide who would rule the valley of the Medway. Horsa was killed and the English withdrew to Sheppey and Thanet. Hengest did not wait long to revenge his brother's death and soon after the fight Kent was an English kingdom.

RAINHAM

The terrifying phantom of Rainham would fit anyone's image of the typical ghost. On the stroke of midnight, on nights of a full moon, a black coach materialises slowly outside the gates of the church of St Helen and St Giles. The coach is driven by a tall man dressed in a voluminous dark cloak, but nobody can tell you what his face is like for he is headless. Also headless are the four jet black stallions which pull the coach. For a few seconds the coach waits, then the figure of a man comes out of the church and walks down the path to the gate. Climbing into the ghastly coach, the man calmly removes his head from his shoulders and holds it in his lap.

Then they are off. The coachman lashes the horses with a whip that cracks as loud as thunder. Breaking into an instant gallop, the horses pull the coach at breakneck speed. Sparks as bright as lightning flash from the horses' hooves as they strike the road. Anyone foolish enough not to get out of the way is blown aside as if stuck by an enormously powerful blast of wind. The air is as hot as a

Rainham church, where a terrifying phantom appears.

furnace or, more likely, as hot as hell.

Careering down the roads and lanes, the coach heads directly for Bloors Place. Charging through the gates, it is last seen lurching wildly over the gardens towards the house, and then vanishes from sight.

This startling manifestation is said to be the coach, attendants and eternally damned spirit of Bad Squire Bloor. Known more properly as Sir Christopher Bloor, this notorious debauchee was the local landowner in the later 16th century. He was infamous for his drunken and riotous lifestyle, which involved the seduction and desertion of local maidens too numerous to mention as well as brawls and punch-ups. The centre of the outrageous events was Bloors Place, where Sir Christopher would throw wild parties for his drinking partners from London, Canterbury and other cities. Women of easy virtue were always invited to sate the desires of the Bad Squire and his mates. On occasions Sir Christopher would set out in his coach to tour the taverns of the area, picking fights and smashing furniture.

When Sir Christopher was found dead in the road outside Bloors Place one morning after a particularly wild night out it was rumoured that he had been murdered by a father of one of the maids he had ruined. But the fact that there was not a mark on his body led to another story, that the Devil had come to Rainham to collect his own.

And so the story of the terrifying coach began. It is a good story, one of the most dramatic in Kent. Almost every account of ghosts in Kent mentions the dreadful coach of Rainham, but nobody can be found who has seen it. Unlike other ghosts, this apparition has no witnesses.

BIGGIN HILL

'Once you have heard it, you never forget,' so said one former RAF pilot of the Spitfire. The 'sewing machine' roar of a Spitfire at full throttle was one of the most distinctive sounds heard at Biggin Hill during the desperate days of the Battle of Britain. And it is still heard there to this day, not only at airshows but also in spectral form.

By June 1940 the German army had carried out Hitler's plans for the conquest of France. Panzer columns had smashed through the French defences, crushed the French armies and driven the British army in France to evacuate through Dunkirk. Hundreds of private yachts and launches had crossed the Channel to help the Royal Navy evacuate the army from the bomb-shattered beaches around Dunkirk. Now Britain stood alone against the might of the seemingly invincible German army. Britain's army was in no shape to fight off an invasion, having left most of its tanks and artillery in France. Hitler ordered his staff officers to draw up plans for invading Britain.

When the German generals produced their plan it was a faultless strategy for armoured panzer columns to race inland, encircle the British army and complete a swift victory. All the generals asked for was transport over the Channel. The German navy, in turn, promised transport but only if they would be safe from air attack. Hitler realised everything depended on control of the air and turned to the bombers, Stukas and fighters of the Luftwaffe to get it for him.

For day after day, week after week, vast formations of German aircraft roared across the Channel to pound the RAF bases, radar stations and key defence sites of southern Britain. In all the Luftwaffe had 2,243 aircraft to throw at Britain, while the RAF had just 650 fighters to defend its airspace.

A key RAF base was the fighter airfield of Biggin Hill, or Biggin on the

Bump as contemporary RAF jargon had it. The Spitfires based here were a major element in the defences of Britain. Fast, agile and armed with eight heavy machine guns, the Spitfires were deadly killing machines as well as being supremely elegant aircraft. Biggin also had a complement of Hurricanes. Slightly slower than the Spitfire, the Hurricane had the same formidable armament and was more robust when it came to taking damage and still remaining airworthy. Together the Spitfire and Hurricane pilots went up on sortie after sortie to protect Britain.

Inevitably there were casualties, and Biggin Hill lost more than most. The Luftwaffe raided the base time and again. Two station commanders were killed along with dozens of ground crew and support staff. But it was the pilots who had the most dangerous job and who were killed in greatest numbers. It is one of these pilots who returns to Biggin Hill in his ghostly craft.

The phantom is never seen, only heard. But it is that unmistakable whirr of a Spitfire at full throttle that roars low over Biggin Hill. The ghost comes at any time of day or night, with nothing before or after to mark its passing. Those who lived here during the Battle of Britain itself claim that the rising and falling of the engine revs indicate the pilot is completing what was known as a "victory roll", a slow roll of the aircraft as it passes at low altitude. A few who have heard the phantom plane when on the airfield itself say they have heard low voices and clinking glasses just after the Spitfire has passed overhead. Perhaps the long lost pilot is coming home to join his colleagues and friends for a victory drink he could never enjoy in life.

The Spitfire mounted near the gates to Biggin Hill Airport. Its ghostly counterpart reminds visitors of the station's heroic wartime past.

A second ghost was highly active in the 1960s, when Biggin Hill was coming to the end of its life as an active RAF station. A figure wearing RAF uniform of the war years was seen striding up to the main gates and passing through without stopping. One sentry who saw the phantom in around 1964 had not been told of the ghost and next morning presented himself at sick parade as suffering from hallucinations. The Medical Officer soon put him right and sent him back on duty.

KEMSING

When it comes to saints and sinners, few places in Kent can touch Kemsing. This charming little village has had more than its fair share of both.

The village begins its history with a saint, and a most engaging one at that. There were Celtic and Roman settlements in the area, but it is with the early English that Kemsing enters the written record as Cimescing, the people of Cimes. In 961 Queen Wulfrith of England gave birth to a daughter. The proud father, King Edgar, named his child Edith and arranged for her to receive the standard education due a noble girl at this time. Even as a child Edith showed great devotion to the worship of Christ and a skill beyond her years in reading the scriptures. She enrolled as a nun at the convent of Wilton where she spent the rest of her life in holy contemplation. After her death she was canonised to become St Edith.

Back in Kemsing, the locals built a little chapel where the saint had been born. Almost at once a spring of water leapt from the ground. The waters were soon found to have miraculous powers and even today are said to be good for the eyes.

It is a sinner, however, who provides the most active ghost in Kemsing. On 29th December 1170 the most brutal murder of Thomas à Becket, Archbishop of Canterbury, was committed in Canterbury Cathedral by four knights from the household of King Henry II of England. It was a murder that would reverberate through the political and ecclesiastical circles of all Christendom.

The church at Kemsing where a phantom comes to beg forgiveness from God.

The story of Becket's murder is well documented. Becket had been born the son of a merchant and had worked his way up to knightly status through hard work, talent and by being a most engaging and entertaining companion. Henry II raised him to high government office during the 1150s and entrusted him with numerous diplomatic and administrative tasks. In 1162 Henry put Becket forward to be Archbishop of Canterbury. Henry reasoned that with his friend in charge of the English Church his numerous disputes with the Church would be quickly solved. But Becket proved to be as loyal to his new employer, the Church, as he had been to his previous employer, the King.

For the next eight years the disputes between Crown and Church became ever more bitter and more personal. Finally in a fit of anger, Henry raged 'Who will rid me of this turbulent priest?' Thinking to win the king's favour, four of his knights at once leapt on to their horses and rode to Canterbury. They found Becket at prayer at the high altar, which they dragged him away from, but they could not get him outside the cathedral. So they hacked him to death on the spot, killing him with a sword blow to the head and using a sword point to scoop out his brains.

When Henry heard the news he was aghast, never having meant any real harm to his old friend. He was forced to cave in to the Church and in 1174 crawled on his knees to the tomb of Becket at Canterbury and did penance for his part in the killing. Becket became the most senior of all the English saints. The knights who had done the actual killing, Hugh de Merville, William de Tracy, Reginald Fitzurse and Richard le Breton were likewise forced to do humiliating penance and were treated as social outcasts.

According to Kent legend, however, one of these knights had repented within minutes of committing the murder. He had ridden out of Canterbury with his colleagues but got no further than Kemsing before his growing guilt overwhelmed him. Pulling aside from the road, the knight rode up to the church of St Mary the Virgin in Kemsing, dismounted and went inside to throw himself prostrate and beg for divine forgiveness.

Which of the knights this was is not recorded, but his ghost still recreates that first craving for absolution. On chill winter evenings the knight rides up to the doors of the church, dismounts and goes within to pray silently and with obvious fervour for forgiveness of his sins.

Five centuries later another sinner came to Kemsing, but this man had no time to repent. We do not know his surname, but he was known to his colleagues as William. During the English Civil War a troop of Cavaliers halted in Kemsing to rest their horses and have a bite to eat, before riding on to attack the Roundheads. The officers withdrew to Watery Lane to discuss their plans. As they talked, they realised that they were being spied upon by a Cavalier named William, who had only recently joined their troop. Taking William to be a Roundhead spy, the Cavaliers strung him up without giving him a chance to explain himself.

Mounting up, the Cavaliers rode off leaving their victim to swing in the air. Whether it was William who sinned by spying or the officers by hanging an innocent man is unknown. But either William or one of his murderers returns to Watery Lane to the scene of his crime. Dressed in opulent dress with a wide lace collar and broad-brimmed hat, this phantom Cavalier stands in moody contemplation of the spot where the unfortunate youth was hanged.

In 1908 another murder most foul was committed here. Retired General Luard set out one day, as usual, to walk to his golf club at Godden Green. His wife accompanied him as far as the woods, before turning back for home. When General Luard returned some time later he found a friend in the garden unable to get in and no sign of his wife. Her body was later found in the woods with a single gunshot wound to the head. The General had plenty of witnesses to swear he was at the golf club at the time of the murder, but local gossip blamed him for the killing. A few weeks later he killed himself and the woods have had a sinister reputation ever since.

Quite what the holy St Edith would have made of such mayhem and murder is best left not mentioned.

WROTHAM

The laughing ghost of Wrotham is no jovial fellow, but a chilling and terrifying ghost. Fortunately he has not been seen for some years, though there is always the chance that he might reappear. The haunting is notable for becoming the subject of one of the earliest serious attempts to investigate a ghost.

The phantom in question walked at Wrotham House in the years before World War I. He was dressed in a fine grey three piece suit of late 18th century cut and edged with elegant silver lace. His usual walk was along a corridor, up a flight of stairs and into a bedroom at the rear of the house. Once in that room he would laugh, but there was no humour in the sound. Instead it was a cold and evil laugh, as if he were planning some crime and gaining much enjoyment from the anticipation of it.

He was, indeed, an evil man. This ghost is that of a former owner who had murdered his own brother as he slept in the haunted bedroom. Perhaps the cold laugh was given as he bent to his work that night but the deed proved fatal to both brothers, for the killer was hanged for his crimes.

The haunting was thoroughly investigated in the 1870s by the Lord Halifax of the day. He questioned a Mrs Brooke and her maid, Miss Page, who had both seen this unpleasant ghost. Lord Halifax gathered details about the ghost and his appearance as well as the story behind the haunting. Unlike other amateur investigators of his day, however, Halifax went further and made determined efforts to look beyond the haunting, trying to fathom the science behind it.

Halifax took as his starting point that neither Mrs Brooke nor her maid knew anything about the haunting before seeing the ghost, both of them being only visitors to the house. This meant they were unlikely to have dreamed about or had hallucinations of the ghost after having been told about it. Whatever they saw had been unprompted by stories of the phantom. He also insisted that both ladies be willing to put their names to their experiences in public, thus escaping the charge that he was having his leg pulled by anonymous friends.

The village sign of Wrotham, where one of the earliest proper investigations into a haunting took place over a century ago.

One interesting point that emerged from the investigation was that the maid was in the habit of wedging a chair under the door handle whenever she slept in a strange house. She had seen the ghost open the door and enter her room, yet when she herself tried to leave the room the chair was still firmly in place. This might mean that the ghost had only temporarily disturbed the door and chair, effectively creating a local and short-lived disturbance. On the other hand the door may never have actually opened, meaning the maid may have imagined the whole scene or may have perceived a vision which had no real physical presence.

Another feature Lord Halifax noted in this case was that the room had become suddenly very cold just before the ghost appeared and did not warm up again until a few minutes after it had gone. As stated earlier, this drop in temperature has since been noted by many investigators into ghosts and the paranormal. It is not merely a perceived chill felt by witnesses, but has been recorded by scientific instruments in haunted rooms. One theory holds that whatever it is that causes ghosts to appear draws its energy from the surroundings. As that energy is sucked away the temperature falls dramatically. It is, of course, just a theory but it does fit the facts.

Lord Halifax investigated a number of hauntings and put his findings together in a book entitled, predictably enough, *Ghost Stories*. Although by the standards of modern day psychic investigators Lord Halifax was rather clumsy and unscientific in his methods, he did set an example of subjecting ghosts and hauntings to rather more exhaustive treatment than the mere recounting of fireside horror tales.

MEREWORTH

Friday the 13th is generally reckoned to be an unlucky day. It was certainly very unlucky for one Jack Diamond, a highwayman who made using the roads of northern Kent rather dangerous in the late 18th century.

Diamond was not this criminal's real name. That has long been forgotten by both history and legend. Young Jack gained his name by wearing a large and showy diamond ring on his right hand. It was one of the first things that he stole on the open road and he kept it as a sort of talisman. It did him no good at all one Friday 13th when he was at home in his cottage just south of Mereworth, near to West Peckham. Early that morning, about dawn, a sudden and ferocious fire burst out in the cottage. What started the fire is a mystery, but it was the end of Jack Diamond and his career on the road.

Jack Diamond still roams, however. Dressed in a tricorn hat and a long cloak, he returns to the site of his misfortune on most Friday the 13ths, usually early in the morning.

The haunted lane south of Mereworth.

HOLLINGBOURNE

The two ghosts of Hollingbourne could not be more different. One is gentle and unassuming, the other dramatic and startling in the extreme.

The first ghost is that of Lady Grace Gethin, who died there just over three hundred years ago. The day before she died Grace was attending a Communion service at the parish church when she fell into a trance. After two hours the young woman came to with a tale to tell so remarkable that a stone was set up on the church wall to record the event. 'She was vouchsafed in a miraculous manner an immediate prospect of her future blisse for ye space of two houres to ye astonishment of all about her and being like St Paul in an inexpressible transport of joy thereby fully evidencing her foresight of the heavenly glory in inconceivable raptures triumphing over death and continuing sensible to ye last she resigned her pious soul to God and victoriously entered rest.'

Lady Grace's rest has not proved to be as serene as might have been expected from her vision of God in glory. Her ghost is a regular visitor to the churchyard, walking from the lychgate to her tomb.

Nor did Lady Grace's reputation for sanctity remain undisturbed. As they cleared up her possessions, Grace's family found a collection of notebooks and papers on which their young daughter had written down poems, thoughts and essays. The writings were both moving and mature, showing a grasp of Christian teachings, charitable love and holy devotion which was remarkable in such a young girl. The collected writings were published and proved to be an immediate success, selling in huge numbers. Only then was it realised that the writings were almost exclusively by other writers, Lady Grace had merely copied them out in her own handwriting for future reference. She remains, nevertheless, a young lady who was obviously imbued with a degree of holiness quite unusual at the time.

The church at Hollingbourne is graced by the ghost of a gentle and kind lady, very different to the wild young man who gallops his horse down nearby lanes.

The other phantom at Hollingbourne goes by the ominous name of the Wild Rider. Mounted on a black stallion of ferocious looks, the Wild Rider appears in daylight hours from out of nowhere, towards the northern end of the village, and gallops at breakneck speed up the hill towards Hollingbourne House. Though the horse is racing flat out with nostrils flared and ears laid back, the rider urges the beast on to greater and greater speeds, lashing his mount with whip and raking it with his spurs. Clearly there is some great desperation driving the man on at such frenzied pace. The Wild Rider gallops on without pause until he reaches the gates of Hollingbourne House where he suddenly vanishes. Eerily the entire performance is carried out in dead silence.

At night, it is a very different story. Once darkness falls the Wild Rider is not seen, but the pounding hooves of the horse and the cursed oaths of the rider urging ever greater speed are heard quite clearly.

It is thought that this might be the ghost of a young man named Duppa who lived at Hollingbourne House around 200 years ago. He was a lover of fine horses and was a rider of great skill. He did, however, allow his ambitions to get the better of him. Returning from a gallop on a new purchase he tried to jump the gates to his house, but the horse fell and young Duppa died of a broken neck.

LEEDS CASTLE

The magnificent castle at Leeds is one of the most beautiful in England and one of the oldest in the country. It has a formidable reputation for being haunted not by just one ghost, but by two.

The Black Dog of Leeds is one of the more famous spectral animals in Kent and there are many tales associated with it. Most stories link the Black Dog with doom and disaster. 'It brings bad luck to the person who sees it,' declared one local confidently, 'and it means bad luck up at the Castle as well.'

According to the locals, the Black Dog of Leeds is linked to another supernatural resident of Leeds Castle, a 15th-century Duchess of Gloucester. This lady was found guilty of witchcraft, heresy and necromancy at a time when the Church and civil courts alike treated such crimes with utmost severity. Being aunt to King Henry VI, however, saved the lady's life and she was sentenced to life imprisonment instead of death. She was brought to

Leeds, for it was believed the castle offered a suitable level of comfort for the duchess, as well as strict security.

The wicked duchess had been in residence only a few months when the Black Dog began to roam the surrounding countryside. It was widely reported that this spectral hound was the evil familiar of the witch. The duchess, it was said, sent the dog out to be her eyes and ears in the locality, and to report back to her on what was going on beyond the walls of her prison. No wonder the good folk of Kent gave the Black Dog of Leeds a wide berth when they came across it.

Although the legend has grown that bad luck follows

One of the lanes near Leeds Castle which is haunted by a gigantic black hound.

in its wake, this is not true for everyone. In the mid-19th century a lady guest at the castle was sitting alone on a bench which backed onto the ancient walls. Seeing a large black dog lollop by, she got up to follow it. She had taken no more than half a dozen steps when a stone cornice crashed down from the walls to crush the bench where she had been sitting. If she had not moved she would have been injured, perhaps killed. Maybe the infamous phantom hound had taken a liking to her.

Leeds Castle was old even when the wicked duchess was imprisoned there. It takes its name from a nobleman named Leedian who built a house on the

Many stories circulate about the beautiful Leeds Castle, but only one ghost has any claim to reality, that of a lady with long dark hair.

site back in the 9th century. In those distant days Kent was still an independent kingdom, not joining the rest of England until forced to do so in response to the Viking invasions. Leedian's home was a comfortable wooden hall with stables and associated agricultural buildings. Not until the Normans came was the house turned into a castle. In 1278 it was bought by Eleanor of Castile, queen to King Edward I, and thereafter remained a favourite country retreat of the Queens of England until Tudor times. Most of the present castle dates to the extensive rebuilding carried out by Queen Eleanor, though it was substantially renovated in Victorian times.

HARRIETSHAM

The phantom which haunts the Ringlestone Arms just north of Harrietsham is something of a mystery. Nobody knows who he is or when he lived, even less why he haunts this fine 17th century pub.

Although the ghost is never seen, the heavy sound of boots makes it undoubtedly a man. The nature of the stomping indicates that the ghost in question is both heavy and possessed of impressively robust footwear. The haunting always follows the same pattern. It comes late at night, often after closing time. The footsteps are heard tramping about in the main cellar underneath the bar. The ghost moves about purposefully with measured tread, then makes for the narrow, ladder-like stairs that climb up to the bar. With determined stomps, the ghost climbs the stairs one at a time. Reaching the

The Ringlestone Arms, just north of Harriestsham, is haunted by a most mysterious phantom.

topmost stair the ghost stops. There is a moment's silence, followed by a loud thump coming from the cellar floor, as if the invisible ghost had thrown a heavy object down the hatch.

The ghost has been heard frequently and by several different persons and has been pursuing his bizarre mission since at least the 1960s. Quite what he is doing remains a baffling mystery.

TONBRIDGE

The pub in Tonbridge known as the Cardinal's Error takes its name from the fact that this was formerly a farmhouse belonging to Cardinal Thomas Wolsey in the 16th century, and from a fatal mistake the powerful churchman made here. Wolsey was born the son of an Essex butcher in 1475 but his keen intellect won him a scholarship to Oxford where he studied at Magdalen College and won himself a Fellowship. His outstanding learning and administrative ability offered him the pick of posts at Oxford, but instead Wolsey chose to become the Secretary to the Archbishop of Canterbury.

It was this post that brought him to Tonbridge. Wolsey was not just skillful and talented, he was also extremely ambitious. He used his position in Canterbury to acquire for himself the rents and deeds of various Church property. One of the rents he acquired was that paid for farmland by the priory at Tonbridge. The guest lodgings at the priory were comfortable and the monks were willing to turn a blind eye to Wolsey's taste for luxury. Tonbridge became a favourite retreat for the rising star.

In 1507 Wolsey left the employment of the Archbishop for that of King Henry VII, but he managed to keep his hands on the lands he had acquired. Two years later the pleasure-loving Henry VIII came to the throne. Wolsey's ambitions now had no limits. While the dashing young king spent his time organising parties, playing sports and chasing women, Wolsey was gathering the reins of power into his own hands. And he was helping himself to a large amount of wealth while he was about it. In 1513 he became Bishop of Lincoln and the following year Archbishop of York. A year later he was created a cardinal by the Pope.

It was while at Tonbridge that Wolsey accepted the post of Papal Legate. This was to prove a disastrous move as, under English law, a servant of the Crown could not accept a post which made him the servant of a foreign ruler. In his rise to power and wealth, Wolsey had made many enemies as he haughtily wielded royal power and stripped lands of their wealth. Those enemies now moved. They persuaded King Henry VIII that Wolsey was working for himself and others, not for England or the king, and used his acceptance of the post of Legate as proof. In 1529 Wolsey

The door in Tonbridge's Cardinal's Error which is frequently thrown open and slammed shut by the resident ghost.

was arrested and a date set for his trial. Broken and sick, Wolsey gave up the will to live and died before his trial could take place.

The pub named for Wolsey's mistake is now the home to some odd hauntings, including footsteps which pace up and down the upstairs corridor. Is this the Cardinal restlessly mulling over his fatal decision? It might be. On the other hand the pacing might be the footsteps of the charming young lady in a large hat who haunts the bar downstairs. The ghost is described as wearing clothes of the Georgian period, with a wide crinoline dress, but it is her wide-brimmed hat with its sweeping feather which is her most noticed feature.

This is Nellie, the phantom of a poor farm girl who lived here some centuries back. She was made pregnant by a local man who promised her marriage and his fortune, before jilting her. Nellie dressed herself in her wedding finest and then drowned herself in the pond that lay behind the pub, where a new housing estate was built in the 1970s. She is seen most often walking up to the pub from the old pond site, throwing the door open, slamming it shut and walking across the bar. She disappears through the door that leads to the private stairs, presumably to go up to her old bedroom.

Nellie occasionally gets up to some mischief. She is particularly fond of a spot in the bar and will often twist the wall light at an angle overnight or move the furniture around so that what was tidy becomes a jumble. When she gets up to such tricks, all that is needed is for the person who finds the mess to say clearly and firmly 'Nellie. We live here now. This is not your home any longer.' The trouble will then cease for a few months. But Nellie always returns.

HEVER

Hever is a tiny village which boasts a fine castle and impressive church. The church of St Peter dates from the 14th century and is graced by some impressive stonework and fine architecture. It also has the tombs of the local Boleyn family which owned the 13th century castle for generations. It is the best known Boleyn, Anne, who haunts this charming place.

The Boleyns were a wealthy family and well-connected enough for Sir Thomas to marry Elizabeth Howard, daughter of the Earl of Norfolk in around 1500. Their daughter, Anne, was brought up at Hever before being sent to stay at the French court at the age of fifteen to gain a continental sophistication. When the darkly attractive young Anne returned to England in 1521 it at first seemed she would marry Henry Percy, the heir to the fabulously wealthy Earl of Northumberland. But then another Henry, the king, took an interest.

At first Anne did not encourage the King's passion. Henry VIII was married to Catherine of Aragon and young Anne clearly preferred to be the virtuous wife of a nobleman than the mistress of a king. But in 1527 Henry began divorce proceedings against Catherine. Sensing she could become queen, Anne joined her relatives in careful manoeuvring to get the king to choose her as his next wife, rather than opt for a foreign dynastic alliance. In January 1533, with the royal divorce complete, Henry and Anne were married. Later that year Anne gave birth to the baby girl who would later be Queen Elizabeth I. A number of failed pregnancies were followed by the birth of a stillborn son in 1536.

By this time King Henry's passion for Anne had cooled and he had moved on to other mistresses. The queen's failure to provide a male heir to the throne began to be a serious problem. Henry had no brothers or close male relatives to inherit his throne and if he died without a son the Crown would pass out of his family. England might well plunge into a renewed round of civil war like the murderous Wars of the Roses which had ended barely a generation earlier. Anne was now in her thirties, an age when childbirth was precarious in the 16th century.

Worried about his heir and no longer in the throes of love, Henry began to listen to gossip spread by enemies of the Boleyn and Howard families. He also began to notice a young woman named Jane Seymour. In May 1536 Henry ordered the arrest of his Queen on charges of adultery, and five men with

The gatehouse to Hever Castle, through which rides the ghost of Anne Boleyn, returning to her childhood home after her brutal execution.

whom she had supposedly shared her bed were accused of high treason. The secret trial that followed did little to discover the truth, but accepted gossip and rumour as fact and gave the guilty verdict Henry wanted. On 19th May Anne was executed, as were her supposed lovers.

Within days the shade of Anne Boleyn was seen at Hever Castle. The body of the dark-haired beauty was carried home in a coach and four which rattled over the bridge across the River Eden and into the grounds of the castle. In the days that followed the ghost was seen wandering happily around the grounds of her childhood home. Anne Boleyn had come home.

The shade of the short-lived queen has been seen around Hever ever since. The grounds were extensively remodelled in the 1900s by the American millionaire William Waldorf Aster who turned them into an Italianate garden to show off his impressive collection of Classical sculptures. The change has done nothing to disturb Anne Boleyn. She still wanders gently around the grounds as if reliving happier days of her youth.

The road outside the castle is the territory of a much less gentle phantom. This ghost is that of an 18th century farmer who rages and stomps around in a great temper. Well he might. This unfortunate man in thick woollen working clothes and a floppy brimmed hat was murdered here for the money he was carrying back from market and his killer never brought to justice.

ROYAL TUNBRIDGE WELLS

It is a very modern ghost that is to be met in the town centre of Tunbridge Wells. Identified variously as a Rolls Royce, a Bentley or a Daimler, this large and impressive phantom motor car is pure white with gleaming chrome and dark, tinted windows. Those who see this modern mechanical ghost say that it conveys an overwhelming sense of money, wealth and comfort when it glides past. Big and expensive cars can easily create such an impression without being in any way supernatural, but there is something about this vehicle which demands that it be looked at. Having attracted notice, the powerful car pulls up at the side of the road as if to park. It then shimmers and shakes as if it were a reflection in wind-ruffled water. Then it is suddenly gone.

Just outside the town centre, where the Broomhill Road takes a sharp turn, there appears a ghost of a man who seems to date from the 1920s or 1930s, the same period as the car. He wears an expensive looking grey suit and the sort of wide-brimmed hat that was fashionable back then. The man seems to be waiting for a vehicle because he peers carefully at passing cars and vans. Eventually he sees one that clearly takes his fancy for some reason. He then raises his hand as if waving to a friend and promptly vanishes.

Whether he has anything to do with the limousine is unlikely. But it is intriguing to wonder what would happen if the ghostly man in grey ever waved down the phantom limousine.

BAYHAM ABBEY

The beautiful ruins of Bayham Abbey stand almost on the border with Sussex, close to the village of Little Bayham. Lying, as they do, in the sheltered and heavily wooded valley of the River Teise, the ruins have a picturesque quality that makes them among the most charming in England.

The beauty of Bayham Abbey is no accident. In the late 18th century the ruins were made the centrepiece of a landscape garden by the famous designer Humphrey Repton, pupil of the great 'Capability' Brown. Repton did, however, have the sense not to alter the ruins themselves too much. The north transept, cloisters and a pair of chapels remain, but the rest of this once sprawling complex has been reduced to mere foundations.

Perhaps predictably the ghosts of Bayham are monks. There is nothing remotely threatening about these gentle ghosts. There are about a dozen phantom monks, who form up in procession to move around the cloisters and into what remains of the church. Moving in pairs, the monks walk up what was once the centre of the choir to the site of the high altar, where they vanish.

This impressive procession occurs only at dusk, or soon after darkness has settled on the ruins. The ghosts have no light of their own, so if they appear after dark they are seen only if the moon is out.

The peaceful ruins of Bayham Abbey, haunted by some equally peaceful phantoms.

The abbey is now in the care of English Heritage, which closes the ruins to the public well before nightfall. It is therefore unlikely that a modern visitor will see the full panoply of the monks in procession. But that does not mean that no supernatural activity is likely. The scent of incense has been reported many times by visitors to the ruins.

Rather less often heard are the sounds of a choir singing simple choral works. The sound is always faint, as if it is coming from a great distance. English Heritage sometimes stages concerts against the romantic backdrop of the ruins and some have mistaken the phantom singing for modern musicians preparing for an event. Needless to say, no living choirs have been on hand when the phantom choir has been heard.

In passing it is worth noting that Bayham Abbey did not share the fate of so many others by being abolished by King Henry VIII during the Reformation. It had already been disbanded and its property sold by Cardinal Wolsey a decade before the break with the Roman Church. The motive was purely financial, not religious. Wolsey was looking for funds for his Christ Church College at Oxford, and the rich lands of Bayham were sold to contribute to this.

• The East •

HARTY

The Isle of Harty is now linked by very solid land to the Isle of Sheppey and no longer deserves the classification as an island. It was not always like this, however.

The low valley fringing Harty to the north was once a wide marsh, broken by narrow twisting streams and pools of dark, peaty water. This was a lonely, eerie place. When the chill wind blew through the reeds and dank vegetation, the area seemed almost other worldly. Perhaps that is how the place got its name. In Old English, Harty derives from a phrase which, in modern parlance, might be loosely rendered as 'The Marsh of Monsters'.

Intriguingly, the name is fairly close to the name Heorot, the great hall plagued by a man-eating monster in the ancient English poem *Beowulf*. The topography of the Heorot in the poem closely matches that of the area around Harty. The cliffs on the east coast of Sheppey shine when wet, as do those in the poem, and it is possible to ride a horse down them, though only just. Other similarities are numerous, and the history of this region makes it likely that Harty was an off-shore English stronghold off a Romano-British mainland about the time the poem was composed.

It is an intriguing possibility that the Marsh of Monsters in this isolated area of Kent might have been the inspiration for some of the most ancient literature in the English language. Whatever the truth of this, the monsters have not been seen since the marshes were drained some generations ago.

One of the few remaining patches of undrained marsh on the Isle of Harty –
once notorious as the Marsh of the Monsters.

FAVERSHAM

The phantom sailor of Faversham is an impressive spectacle. Close your eyes and imagine an old-time sailor and it is likely you will be visualising the intimidating figure that roams the foreshore.

The ghost is seen most often in and around the old Shipwright's Arms, which lies beside a tidal creek running off the River Swale. In days gone by, when small sailing craft carried fruit, shellfish and other produce from Kent up to London, the Swale was a favoured refuge in spells of bad weather. If high seas or strong winds threatened, the little ships would put into the Swale and drop anchor until a fair wind blew again. It seems that the ghostly sailor is the legacy of one such ship that did not quite make it.

Late one stormy night this sailor was found slumped a few yards from the door of the pub. His muddy footsteps led back to the foreshore and the Swale beyond. The weather was dreadful, but none of those who braved the elements could see any vessel in the sheltered waters. The sailor himself died soon afterwards without recovering his senses and the next day wreckage was washed up to show that a small vessel had foundered the night before. No other survivors were found so where the ship had come from remained a mystery.

It was surmised that the sailor had somehow got ashore from the stricken vessel and had made his way towards the welcoming lights of the pub before collapsing from exhaustion.

It would seem that the ghost now recreates his failed mission to summon help for his stricken ship. He comes up from the creek, staggering over the mud flats, on dark and blustery winter nights. As the ghost approaches the pub his

The Shipwright's Arms on the outskirts of Faversham, near which has been seen a phantom sailor with staring eyes.

step becomes firmer and stance more upright. As he reaches the front door, the ghost pushes it open and strides in. Then he vanishes as if a light had been switched off.

Witnesses describe the sailor as being a tall, broad man dressed in an old-fashioned and dark coloured reefer jacket. His hair is long and dark, tied back into a plait or ponytail. With him he brings a strong stench of tobacco and rum, which is only right considering his profession. His eyes are red and wide, and it is these that seem to be his most noticeable feature. Some describe how he glares at them, others that he stares sightless in front of him, still more that his eyes look as if he has been weeping.

Who the phantom sailor was and where he came from will

A yacht rides gently at anchor on the Swale near Faversham. Some years ago a savage storm led to a tragic shipwreck here – and so to a very persistent haunting.

never be known. But he must have cared deeply for those whom he left behind on his doomed ship for his endless mission to save them continues generations after he first failed in the attempt.

MARGATE

The Theatre Royal at Margate was, in its day, one of the finest in England. Once the railway was built vast crowds of Londoners came down to Margate on day trips, weekend breaks and extended holidays. They brought with them pockets bulging with money to spend and long leisure hours in which to spend them. The large, 2,000 seat Theatre Royal was one of the places they came to spend that money.

The actor-manager here was the redoubtable Sarah Thorne who had been a big name on the London stage before she bought the Margate theatre in 1874, and established a company of leading actors which put on some of the finest performances in the kingdom. Miss Thorne worked tirelessly. She not only supervised the productions but acted in them herself. She would also be on hand to welcome any guests of quality and went out of her way to tempt to her theatre any famous people visiting the town.

The Theatre Royal at Margate, home to more than one haunting.

By 1899 the theatre was enjoying great critical acclaim as well as commercial success. Unfortunately, this was when Miss Thorne died suddenly at the relatively early age of 62. Soon afterwards the theatre lost its leading actors and reputation and the place slowly deteriorated, becoming little more than a not very good provincial rep.

It was not to be expected that

51

the doughty Miss Thorne could tolerate such a decline. Before long her ghost began to roam the building. Throwing open the doors at the rear of the auditorium she would sweep down the central aisle in one of her impressive Victorian evening gowns. As she approached the stage the phantom would raise a hand as if to admonish an actor to do better or to give some stage direction, but would vanish before she spoke a word. So regular had this ghost become by 1914 that it was becoming a nuisance. Despite her best effort, the spectral Miss Thorne could do nothing to halt the decline or her beloved theatre. By the late 1930s the theatre had closed. It has since been a cinema, a furniture store, a warehouse and is now a theatre once more. But Miss Thorne still walks.

She seems oblivious to the fact that there are no actors or stage hands for her to order about. Like most ghosts who seem endlessly to replay events that they knew when alive Miss Thorne takes no notice of the changing times and surroundings, she simply carries on.

There is said to be another ghost in this building, that of an actor who committed suicide in a most dramatic fashion. Having been sacked by the theatre – whether by Miss Thorne or not is unknown – he hired the box which overlooks the stage. Waiting until a quiet moment during that night's performance, the aggrieved actor leapt to his feet, proclaimed his woes to the astonished audience and then leapt to his death.

This ghost is neither seen nor heard. Instead he manifests himself in the form of glowing balls of light that float around above the stage and near to the box from which he leapt. Bobbing about in mid-air these globes of light have been seen on many occasions. The same ghost is also held responsible for the muttering and whispering that sometimes echo down to the auditorium from the direction of the box, now long since blocked off.

RICHBOROUGH

The phantoms which march in Richborough are among the oldest in Kent, indeed some claim them to be among the oldest in Britain. They are certainly among the most elusive.

'I've not seen them in my two years as seasonal custodian,' reported John Grigsby in the summer of 2003. 'But ghostly legionaries do haunt the site.' Mr Grigsby could be forgiven for not having encountered the ghosts during his time at the site. They do not appear very often, perhaps their great age makes them less active than they once were.

But march they most certainly do. The first sign that the Romans are about is the steady tramp of hob-nailed sandals on stone, though both the sandals and the stone road surface are long since gone. Sometimes this is all that shows the ghosts are stirring. But on rare occasions a column of marching men slowly forms. 'It is as if they are marching out of a mist,' reported one witness. 'First you see a vague outline, then a solid silhouette and finally the real thing. And they look real too.' The column of marching men tramps up from the direction of the sea, past the outer walls of the old Roman fortress and on as if marching inland. But then they fade in much the same way as they appeared.

Richborough was closely connected to the Roman army for almost four centuries. It was here that the invasion army of AD 43 landed and hurriedly erected a fortified beachhead. The slight depressions that mark the defensive ditches of this first work can be traced on the ground, but only if you know where to look. It was here that the Emperor Claudius landed to scurry inland for the victory parade, before leaving again just 16 days later to dash back to Rome. By the time Claudius left the first fort was being replaced by a large stores depot. Built of wood, nothing of this now remains.

There are, however, the mysterious remnants of a massive stone construction dating from the Claudian era. For centuries archaeologists and historians have gazed at the oddly shaped stone platform and the scattered fragments of statues and carved mouldings. Not until the last years of the 20th century was the mystery resolved. This was part of a massive triumphal arch which stood around 90 feet high and was topped by a bronze statue of Claudius mounted on a horse. As imperial symbols of conquest go, it was certainly dramatic.

By the 3rd century, barbarian attacks on Britain were becoming increasingly common. The depot at Richborough was transformed into a stone fortress with massive walls and elaborate bastions, on top of which were mounted catapults and other engines of war. The military complex of defended port and fortress became the cornerstone of the British defences in the south, as Hadrian's Wall was in the north. Richborough became the base for the II Legion, one of the premier fighting forces of the Empire. But even these mighty fortifications could not hold back the rising tide of invasion. The legionaries were called back to defend Rome itself and Richborough was abandoned.

It is not entirely clear to which period the phantom legionaries belong. Their style of armour would seem to indicate that they belong to the early decades of Roman rule, perhaps even to the invasion force. But their route

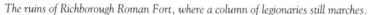

The ruins of Richborough Roman Fort, where a column of legionaries still marches.

follows the line of the road built around the later fortress. They are, however, undoubtedly Roman. The oldest ghosts of Kent march on seemingly for ever.

CANTERBURY

The beautiful city of Canterbury is arguably the oldest inhabited place in Kent, the towns of Dover and Rochester being newfangled Roman settlements a mere 1,900 years old. By the time the Romans came Canterbury was already a thriving town and seat of the King of the Cantiaci, the Celtic tribe which gave its name to both the city and county.

The Romans rebuilt the tribal capital, now known as Durovernum Cantiacorum, and made the city the administrative centre for the surrounding area of south-eastern Britain. They erected stout stone walls around their new city, and these have been patched and repaired over the centuries so that they still form the basis for the city walls that stand today. There was an impressive theatre and several temples as well as splendid town houses decorated with mosaics.

Kent, and therefore Canterbury, was among the first parts of Britain to fall under English rule. The modern coat of arms of Kent, a white horse on a red field, was the symbol of the early English leader Hengest. It was therefore to Kent that the Pope sent his missionaries when he wanted to convert the pagan English to Christianity. In 597 St Augustine arrived and at once established a small church which was to grow to become Canterbury Cathedral. After his death, the Abbey of St Augustine was established in his memory by the rapidly growing Christian population of Kent.

In 1067 the old cathedral was burnt down and the new, much enlarged church that stands today was begun. In 1174 a second fire opened the way for another rebuilding in grand style. Funded by pilgrims coming to Canterbury to pray at the tomb of St Thomas à Becket, England's premier martyr, the new church became one of the largest and finest in Christendom. It is widely admired for its stained glass windows and carvings.

It also has its ghosts, the oldest of which is the phantom of Simon of Sudbury, who was Archbishop in the later 14th century. His ghost has been seen in the aptly named Sudbury Tower on frequent occasions ever since his death – and a most unpleasant death it was too, though he met it bravely enough.

Sudbury was not just Archbishop of Canterbury, he was also the chief finance minister to King Richard II. And as the chief bishop of England he was ultimately responsible for the vast Church lands. In both roles he managed to make himself extremely unpopular. As master of the Church lands he insisted that all rents and fees had to be paid in full and on time. Any defaulters were evicted without mercy. As the King's finance minister he was responsible for the administration of the Poll Tax, a tax levied on each adult in England.

Such exactions on the peasants were made more intolerable by the economic state of the country. The Black Death had decimated the population while a war against France was proving to be a costly failure. In 1380 a new Poll Tax was announced. At a time when the annual wage for a farm labourer was around 13 shillings a year, the tax was set at one shilling per adult. Few people could produce the cash, offering goods instead. Unscrupulous collectors valued the goods at below their true worth, then sold them at market price and pocketed the difference. The peasants were furious at this unfair treatment.

In May 1381 the tax collectors set out to doublecheck some figures that Sudbury had thought suspect, but the people believed a new tax was to be levied. In Kent the collectors behaved with

Canterbury Cathedral, site of at least two hauntings.

astonishing arrogance. When one man said he had paid the two shillings for himself and his wife, the collector demanded another shilling for the man's daughter and to prove the girl was an adult, he lifted her smock. The outraged father knocked the man senseless, then led his fellow villagers to protest to the chief tax collector. The farmer's name was Wat Tyler and his protest quickly grew into the Peasants' Revolt.

Thousands of peasants and farmers followed Wat Tyler to Canterbury. There they broke into the Archbishop's Palace to burn the records of due tax and rent so that they could not be used to implement what the peasants claimed was unfair treatment. The mob, now thousands strong, swept on to London. Tyler managed to keep his followers in order. This was not, after all, meant to be a rebellion but a protest.

The ornate doorway outside Canterbury Cathedral, near which lurks a most unpleasant phantom.

Once in London, however, the crowds got out of hand. On 14th June a mass of protesters found the gates of the Tower of London open and surged inside. The unfortunate Archbishop Simon of Sudbury was in the building at the time. Seeing a horde of rioters thronging through the gates he can have had little doubt of his fate. He dressed himself in his robes and went down to the Tower Chapel to pray. He was still praying when the mob dragged him outside and hacked off his head. A nervous cleric recovered the head and brought it to Canterbury for burial.

Within a matter of days, the ghost of Archbishop Simon was seen walking around his beloved cathedral. In the centuries that have followed since his brutal death, Archbishop Simon has continued to walk the cathedral, appearing in the informal grey cloak that he habitually wore when not on duty. These days, however, he restricts his ghostly wanderings to the Sudbury Tower, where he had his office suite when alive.

The second spectre is altogether more dangerous. This is the phantom of an 18th century servant girl named Nell Cook. The girl waited upon the clergy and fell in love with a Canon. He told her that his mind was devoted to more spiritual matters and did not return her affections. Young Nell was disappointed, but respected the holiness of her beloved. Her bitter heartbreak was therefore mixed with feelings of betrayal a few weeks later when she came in to clean the Canon's rooms and found him in bed with a local woman. She killed them both.

Poor Nell Cook was, of course, hanged for her crime. She was buried under the flagstones close to the door which leads from the Cathedral grounds to the attached King's School. It is here that her ghost walks. It is said to be a most disturbing phantom. The pretty features of the girl are distorted by grief and anguish, turning to anger and hatred. Those who see it are guaranteed to suffer a death in the family within a year and a day of seeing the ghost, or so it is said.

A third ghost has sometimes been seen flitting about in the Norman crypt. The robed figure with a cowl over its head is undoubtedly a monk. It could conceivably date from almost any time since the crypt was built in the 11th century to the time when King Henry VIII abolished the monasteries in the 16th century. Unsurprisingly, however, the figure has been identified as that of St Thomas à Becket, although there does not seem to be any good reason for this other than the fact that he was Canterbury's most famous Archbishop. Becket was martyred above in the main cathedral, however, not in the crypt, and is not known to have had any particular association with the underground chambers.

Becket is also linked, again dubiously, to a pump in Sun Street. It is said that from time to time this pump would produce red water. Legend had it that this was the blood of St Thomas, which the monk was sending to atone for the sins of the citizens of Canterbury. These days the good folk of Canterbury get their water piped in from water treatment works like everyone else and the pump is defunct.

Still in evidence, however, is the cycling Mayor of Canterbury. This worthy supervised the city council in Victorian times and found it quicker and easier to cycle around the city than to walk. The dark-suited figure of the mayor is seen darting down the narrow streets of the old city centre, usually in the winter.

The Marlowe Theatre had a very active, but short lived, ghost in the 1960s. During performances a man in a grey suit would be seen standing in the wings to the right of the stage. Where he came from, nobody knew and none of the staff recognised him. If he was approached, the man would slip behind some scenery or a curtain and could never be found. Even when doors were locked and strict watch was kept, the man in grey would still appear and just as mysteriously vanish.

The events gave rise to some humorous comments about Canterbury having its own Phantom of the Opera. After a few months of regular attendance, the phantom in grey simply stopped appearing.

CHILHAM

Often described as the last medieval village in Kent, Chilham has changed little over the centuries. The charming village square has on one side the richly ornamented 15th century church, on the other the gatehouse to Chilham Castle. Filling the gaps between is a collection of half-timbered houses which seem almost to breathe out an atmosphere of timeless rural England.

The green is also bracketed by a pair of hauntings.

The White Horse Inn is as redolent of old England as any pub in the kingdom. Its half-timbered structure is centuries old and has seen a variety of uses over the years. In the 17th century it was the vicarage to the nearby church of St Mary and was inhabited by Reverend Sampson Horne. Despite the sleepy, peaceful face of the village today, in Reverend Horne's time this little place was at the forefront of national religious upheavals. The Civil War was fought in the 1640s, and was followed by the puritanical dictatorship of Oliver Cromwell. The ban on frivolous Christmas parties and the strict interpretation of the Bible enforced during Cromwell's rule met with the fervent support of Reverend Horne.

But the times were changing. In 1660 King Charles II came back to the throne and with him came a more relaxed attitude to religion and its dogma. Reverend Horne was not best pleased. Fearing his flock would be led astray by the Devil, now that his own brand of Puritanism was no longer enforced, Horne raged from the pulpit about the iniquities of modern life. When he began condemning the new government and the tolerance it allowed in the Church of England, Horne went too far.

Fearing that riots or worse might follow such fiery sermons, the Archbishop of Canterbury moved swiftly to oust the Reverend Horne from the parish of Chilham. Horne may have lost his living, but he had money of his own, so he stayed in the village until his death in 1677, when he was buried in the churchyard. It wasn't long before the spectre of Horne was seen in his old home, which was converted into an inn some years after his death.

The fire of his earthly sermons is long gone and the ghost of the elderly man potters gently around his old home. Most often he is seen sitting comfortably beside the inglenook fireplace on the ground floor. Quite what the enthusiastic firebrand preacher would make of the fact that his one time home is now a public house serving spirits of a very different kind it is best not to imagine. Still, he seems content enough to sit in his chair and watch the customers at their drink and food.

More recently, in the 1960s, a gruesome discovery was made when the White Horse was extended back over the old yard to make space for a new kitchen and dining room. Two skeletons were found just two inches beneath the cobbles. They lay just feet from the boundary of the churchyard and at first it was thought they might be suicides, traditionally not allowed burial in holy ground. Then a local historian found that during the Peasants Revolt of 1381 there had been a fight here in Chilham in which two tax collectors had been

The Inglenook fireplace in the White Horse public house at Chilham
which is the centre for the activities of the phantom vicar.

killed by the furious peasants. These, it is thought, are the skeletons of the hapless pair.

Chilham Castle was for centuries a grim, forbidding fortress which owed its existence far more to stern military necessity than to providing a setting for the happy feasting and jousting so often associated with the medieval period, at least in modern movies. In 1616, the property came into the hands of Sir Dudley Digges. Digges was a wealthy courtier of King James I who wanted a comfortable country seat within easy reach of London. Chilham was ideally situated, but was far from comfortable. Digges pulled down most of the old fortress, though he left the Norman keep, and erected the elegant Jacobean mansion that goes by the name of Chilham Castle today.

In leaving the Norman keep intact, Sir Dudley also left the ghost. This is the phantom of an elegant young lady in medieval dress who flits gently around the staircase. Nobody knows who this ghost is, nor why she haunts the old castle. She is, however, very active. A few years before World War II, a maid was cleaning the stairs. Certain she was alone, the girl turned around to come face to face with the silent ghost. The maid was so startled she stepped back, missed her footing and tumbled down the stairs to fracture her leg. Chilham Castle is now a private home and is not open to the public.

A short distance to the south of the village green is an ancient long barrow. The burial mound dates back around 4,000 years. Local legend has it that it was here, in the valley of the Stour, that the local Celts tried to hold back the Roman invasion of 54BC and that a savage battle raged. Some ancient human bones have been turned up by the plough, which may indicate that some battle occurred here. Although the area is amazingly atmospheric, no ghosts have been reported.

A short distance down the High Street from the square is found the third haunting of Chilham. This is the grey lady who flits around the Woolpack Inn. The management of the Woolpack describe their inn proudly as 'one of the cosiest inns in Kent, if not in England, with a well kept cellar', and they are keen to market their four-poster beds and the traditional decor of their hotel rooms. They are also happy to confirm the presence of their ghost which they describe as 'a resident but friendly ghost'. Indeed, no startling or frightening phenomena have ever been ascribed to this gentle phantom.

BRIDGE

If you are looking for a spectacular ghost, then you should go to Bridge. The name of this village is an ancient one. The oldest known bridge over the River Stour to stand here was built in around AD45 when the invading Romans were constructing a road through the hostile Kent countryside from Dubris, now Dover, to Londinium, now London. Watling Street, as the road became, shared that common characteristic of most Roman roads in running absolutely straight irrespective of local topography. Watling Street became the A2 and, although the village is now bypassed by the modern A2, the old road still runs along its Roman route.

So it is that the road plunges down a steep hill from the south before crossing the Stour by the eponymous bridge and climbing up out of the valley beyond. If ghosts can be taken as evidence of history, then it seems likely that this same route was used by a pre-Roman road. For down this hill there sometimes charges a war chariot of the ancient Celts. Standing in the chariot is a tall man whose cloak streams out behind him as he stands proudly erect, a spear grasped in his hand. In front of the warrior crouches another man who urges on the two ponies which pull the vehicle at a breakneck speed.

Curiously the chariot is seen only from the axle upwards. The bottom half of the wheels and the lower legs of the horses remain firmly below ground level. Perhaps this colourful ghost is still travelling along the level of the old road surface as it was before modern road engineers got to work on it. Charging down the hill, the chariot vanishes into thin air before reaching the river.

The old Roman road which runs down the hill into Bridge and which is haunted by a Celtic war chariot.

The sign outside the Bridge Country Club, which is haunted by a serving maid. The club is private and is not open to the public.

Local legend has it that Julius Caesar fought a battle with the Britons on the banks of the Stour at this point, so perhaps the galloping ghosts recreate some incident in that ancient battle.

Less dramatic and more plaintive is the ghost that haunts the 17th century mansion beside the village. This is the ghost of a serving maid from the time the house was built. The unfortunate girl was seduced by the owner of the house and gave birth to his illegitimate child. The baby died soon after, and local gossip had it that the inconvenient baby had been done to death by its father. Be that as it may, the man refused to pay for a decent funeral and the distraught mother had to carry the tiny corpse from the house in a linen basket. It is this pitiful scene that is recreated in spectral form from time to time.

PATRIXBOURNE

The haunting just outside this little village recalls one of the classics of children's literature in the English language. Higham House was built in 1904 for the colourful Count Louis Zobrowski. The count, son of a Polish aristocrat and American industrial heiress, is now largely forgotten but one of his many inventions has become a legend. It was Zobrowski who designed the famous car Chitty Chitty Bang Bang.

Zobrowski had for years been interested in cars, as had his father before him. He raced Bugattis and competed in both Europe and the USA. Then, in 1920, Zobrowski travelled to Germany to purchase a number of Zeppelin engines no longer needed by the German military after their defeat in World War I. Back at Higham House, Zobrowski bolted one of the 23 litre engines to a Mercedes chassis. He added a four-seater body and complex gearing system before starting the car up and taking to the road outside his house. The monstrously powerful car, with its distinctive

The quiet lane at Patrixbourne where the peace may be shattered by the throaty roar of the phantom racing car known as Chitty Chitty Bang Bang.

sound, swooped out of the driveway and roared through Patrixbourne on a test run. A few months later, Zobrowski again drove the newly named Chitty Chitty Bang Bang through the village on his way to Brooklands race track.

In public for the first time the car astounded all present by powering round the circuit at an average speed of over 100mph. At the next meeting, Zobrowski tore down the final straight at 120mph. Over the following months Zobrowski and his car beat all comers. The car was so fast that it seemed to fly. Together with his team of mechanics, led by Captain Clive Gallop, Zobrowski set new standards of excitement both on and off the track. The mighty Chitty Chitty Bang Bang dominated the race track, while Zobrowski cut a dash with his immaculately tailored clothes and dressed his team in matching outfits and spectacularly coloured caps. With their glamourous parties and race-winning cars, the Zobrowski team became the most envied in the motor racing world.

At the end of 1922 Chitty Chitty Bang Bang was retired from racing and kept by the Count for outings along the country lanes near his home. The deep, throaty roar of the massive engine became a familiar sound around Patrixbourne. Then, in 1924, Zobrowski agreed to drive a new Mercedes car in the Italian Grand Prix at Monza. For some unknown reason, the car careered off the track and Zobrowski was killed. Chitty Chitty Bang Bang was sold to another racing driver who used it a few times, then broke it up for parts.

But the car has returned in spectral form. Not long after reports of Zobrowski's death reached the villagers of Patrixbourne, they again saw him and his mighty car dashing along the lanes around the village. Most often the car thunders down the old A2, turns off to power at high speed to Higham House and swoops into the driveway. It used to be reported that as the car raced up the driveway, the front door would mysteriously open, but that particular manifestation no longer seems to occur.

The car's place in literary history has also been assured. The fame it acquired prompted the author Ian Fleming to use it as the inspiration for the flying car in his children's book of the same name, *Chitty Chitty Bang Bang*.

GOODWIN SANDS

One of the most famous ghosts of Kent is not, strictly speaking in Kent at all. It manifests itself out to sea among the treacherous waters of the Goodwin Sands off the coast near Deal.

On 13th February 1748 the popular local sea captain Simon Peel married one of Deal's society beauties. To celebrate the event he invited 50 guests to join him and his wife on his ship the *Lady Lovibund* on a pleasure cruise out to sea. Unknown to Captain Peel, however, he had a rival in love in the shape of a Mr Rivers. Mr Rivers had been driven mad with jealousy and muttered black oaths of revenge in the days leading up to the wedding, but nobody paid him any attention.

As the wedding party set sail, however, Rivers was seen to slip aboard the ship. While the party was in full swing, the ship was deliberately rammed at full speed on to the deadly Goodwin Sands. It broke up rapidly in the heavy swell which was running at the time and all on board were drowned. Had Rivers deliberately destroyed the craft? It seems likely and is widely held to have been the cause of the disaster.

To the amazement of the many who witnessed the event, the *Lady Lovibund* again set sail from Deal on the afternoon of 13th February 1798, exactly fifty years after the tragedy. As gathering crowds watched, the phantom ship sailed out to sea, put about and again rammed the Goodwin Sands to break up and vanish. Several times since then the ship has been seen dashing through the sea and coming to grief on the Sands. She is usually seen on 13th February, but has sometimes appeared on other dates.

The Goodwin Sands take their name from the powerful Godwin family who held extensive lands and titles in England before the Norman Conquest. The sands were then dry land where the Godwins held manors and grazed livestock. Over the years the land was eroded away until now it emerges above the sea only at exceptionally low tides. The rest of the time the wide sandbank lurks dangerously beneath the waves. These waves are deep enough to prevent the sands from breaking the surface, but shallow enough to entrap the keel of any ship which tries to cross them. A lucky few ships can be refloated, but in heavy seas any craft which strikes the Goodwins is smashed to pieces by the waves, just as was the hapless *Lady Lovibund*. Dozens, perhaps hundreds, of craft have ended their days on the deadly Goodwin Sands.

The *Lady Lovibund* is not the only ghost ship to cruise these waters. The passenger liner SS *Montrose* went down here in 1914 and has become the centre of several stories. The *Montrose* was a 5,000 ton iron-hulled steamship built for the Canadian Pacific Railroad Company in the later 19th century. She spent most of her career sailing entirely blameless and routine voyages from Liverpool to Montreal. In 1910 she set off on what promised to be yet another uneventful voyage but instead found her name plastered across the headlines of the world.

Just a day out of port the captain of the *Montrose*, Henry Kendall, noticed that one of his passengers was behaving rather oddly. A Mr Robinson seemed to be somewhat over familiar with a boy who identified himself as Robinson's nephew, a boy who seemed remarkably feminine. Not only that but Robinson did not respond when his name was called out. When a crew member found a revolver in Robinson's room, Captain Kendall decided to take action. Using the then newfangled invention of wireless radio, Kendall sent a description of his two suspicious passengers to his head office. A few hours later he received a reply informing him that the *Montrose* would be met on arrival in Canada by a squad of armed policemen. It transpired that 'Mr Robinson' was none other than a Dr Hawley Crippen who was wanted for the murder of his actress wife. The 'nephew' turned out to be Crippen's young lover, Ethel Leneve, for whom he had committed the murder. It was the first time that a criminal had been tracked down by radio.

The treacherous waters of the Goodwin Sands, seen from Deal Beach.

As Crippen was dragged away to hang he turned on Kendall and cursed both him and his ship.

The curse seemed empty for soon afterwards Kendall was promoted to command the larger and more luxurious liner SS *Empress of India*. But then the new ship struck a collier in fog and sank with great loss of life.

The *Montrose* fared little better. When Britain went to war with Germany in 1914 she was commandeered by the Royal Navy. Unlike other liners, the *Montrose* was not converted into a troop ship. Instead she was filled with rocks, concrete and ballast and ordered to steam to Dover, where she was to act as a sunken defence against German U-boats. She never got to Dover. As the *Montrose* was being towed past Deal the tow ropes snapped and she drifted towards the Goodwins. Driven on by waves and wind, the *Montrose* struck the Goodwins broadside on. Her back broke and she sank, upright into the shallow seas just off the sands. The Admiralty marked the wreck as a hazard to shipping, but left her intact. The mast of the ship remained above the waves until it snapped off in a storm in 1963. Even now the ship can be seen at very low tides.

She can be seen also on stormy evenings when the wind blows from the south, just as it did on the evening when she sank. The liner is seen to drift sideways on to the Goodwins, to strike home with a distinct judder, then gradually to fade from view.

A third ghost ship on the Goodwins is HMS *Shrewsbury*, a square-rigged warship of the late 18th century. She was wrecked here and has apparently been seen, though not recently.

KINGSTON

The Black Robin Inn is a welcoming sort of a place. So much so that one of its guests has never left. To judge by his dashing outfit, this phantom gentleman must have visited the inn when alive sometime around the 1750s. Unlike many ghosts, the identity of this phantom is known beyond doubt. He is Black Robin, one of the infamous highwaymen of the time, and after whom the pub is now named.

This particular highwayman was clever enough to know how to stay one step ahead of the law. He carried out his crimes on the Dover Road, now the A2, but preyed only on strangers to the area and in particular on foreigners. If he recognised a local among the passengers on a coach he would ride off without robbing it. As a result the local folk had no real incentive to bother themselves with bringing Black Robin to justice. Indeed, given his free-spending habits in local inns, shops and tailors the good folk of the Kingston area gained much from Black Robin's activities.

Black Robin also had a romance with the innkeeper's daughter. The pair were devoted to each other. The forces of law caught up with him eventually, however, and the highwayman was taken away to his fate. It was a bad day in Kingston. He was hauled away to answer for his crimes on the scaffold and his body was hung in chains from a gibbet at the crossroads a few hundred yards south of the tavern where he had spent so much of his time. The distraught young girl shut herself up in the cellar for days, weeping for her dead lover. She died of a broken heart soon afterwards.

The highwayman did not stay away from Kingston for long. Late one night his spectre was seen to ride up to the inn from the direction of the gibbet and dismount. He led his horse into the stables, and then strode through to the bar and vanished. Soon after came the sound of weeping from the cellar. It seems the lovers have both returned to the tavern where they were so happy together in life in order to be together as spectres.

Debbie, the landlady in 2003, takes the stories seriously. She has dressed a tailor's dummy in the clothes of a dashing highwayman and placed him beside the bar, where he stands pint in hand. 'We've not been here long,' said Debbie. 'The only part of the haunting we've had so far is Black Robin riding into the yard and his horse stamping its hooves on the stones. Several people have heard that. And others have heard the girl crying in the cellar, but not when we were actually here. The bit I'm waiting for is when Black Robin comes into the bar and starts living it up with his mates. The landlady before me says that they can get quite rowdy and noisy. Like her we sleep upstairs. She said that Black Robin woke her up more than once with his laughing, singing and chatting. On one occasion she leaned out of bed, hammered her shoe on the

The Black Robin pub at Kingston is said to be haunted by a highwayman and his girlfriend.

floor and shouted at them all to shut up and be quiet. Amazingly they did. She said that scared her worse than the ghostly noises.'

Near the pub is a narrow stream which is usually little more than a muddy trickle but has the habit of sometimes bursting into flood. This is the Nailbourne which was once the centre of a bitter dispute between the gods. Kent was a pagan land before St Augustine was sent here by Pope Gregory I in 596 to convert the heathen English. Augustine received a warm welcome from the King of Kent, Athelbert, whose wife was a Frankish Christian named Bertha. Augustine was given permission to preach Christianity in Kent, but was given little official help.

Typical of his problems were events when he came to Kingston. At the time this area was suffering from a drought which was drying up the fields and threatening both crops and livestock. Having patiently listened to the good monk's preaching, the locals asked if his new god could offer them anything in

The figure of a highwayman who stands in the bar of the Black Robin as dashing and dramatic as the ghost he represents.

the way of practical help, like some water, for instance. Augustine bent down to pray, remaining in silent communion with Christ for some time.

When Augustine stood up, water began to well up from his kneeprints, gradually collecting to form a muddy pool and then flowing off as the Nailbourne. The grateful locals hailed Augustine as a miracle worker and fell to praising Christ and the new religion. The pagan gods were not pleased and came roaring down to Kingston in ferocious temper to raise more water than ever before seen in the village. They caused disastrous floods to sweep the valley, while howling winds tore up trees and blew down houses. Augustine turned back to the valley and again fell to prayer. With Christ's help the saint mastered the pagan gods, but was unable to defeat them entirely. Instead he curbed their power so that the Nailbourne would be a useful and beneficial stream for six years on end, but would flood every seventh year.

These days the stream may not flood quite as regularly as the story might suggest, but the ancient gods return to Kingston every now and then to prove that, although mastered, they are not yet conquered. The Nailbourne flooded most recently in 2002.

BARHAM

The sleepy village of Barham lies astride the Roman road from Dover to Canterbury. Around the village lie open downs which roll gently above the valley of the Nailbourne.

Barham has not always been as relaxing a place as it now appears. The proximity of open downland to the old Roman road has long made this a favoured camping ground for armies. The Romans themselves camped here on their way inland to conquer Britain, and William the Conqueror stopped here after the Battle of Hastings. King John camped here before invading France, as did the Grand Old Duke of York of nursery rhyme fame. Royalists, roundheads, rebel barons and loyal militia have all camped here.

The lychgate outside Barham church, where a gentle lady phantom has often been seen to wander.

The downs above Barham have always been a conspicuous place to gather. Among the many relics of years gone by are a collection of ancient burial mounds which date back over 3,000 years. Local legend has it that one of these burial mounds contains a statue made of pure gold. Legend does not state which mound contains this treasure, although King Henry VIII was sufficiently interested in the story that when he passed by he chose one of the mounds and ordered it to be excavated. He was delighted to find a long-buried suit of armour embellished with gold, but this turned out to be mere gold-plating.

Whether Barham's ghost is linked to any of the armies, kings or noblemen who have stayed here is not entirely clear. She is a gentle soul who walks sedately through the churchyard of the ancient church of St John the Baptist. The church was begun in the 9th century, though most of what stands today was erected in 12th and 14th centuries. It is a large church for the size of the village and was once the parish church for Lord Kitchener of Khartoum, who lived in nearby Broome Park.

WYE

Glamour is not a word usually associated with ghosts, but at Wye there is a phantom that brings a very definite dash of beauty and excitement to the supernatural.

This particular ghost is that of an attractive young blonde who walks the road that leads up White Hill near Wye. Dressed in a long brown coat of expensive cut, the lady seems to date back to no earlier than the 1960s and may be of even more recent date. Like a few other roadside phantoms she has the alarming habit of walking straight out into the path of oncoming traffic. Unlike other jay-walking spectres, this ghost does not vanish at the moment of impact. Instead she remains visible as the vehicle ploughs through her, which is most alarming.

One motorist who encountered this ghost in January 2000 admitted to shaking like a leaf as he slammed the brakes on and brought his car to a halt. He said he had heard the sickening thump as her body hit his car. As usual with such ghosts there was no sign of blood or injured person after the incident.

Having a collision with a person is distressing enough. When that person vanishes into thin air it must be doubly alarming. But the beautiful woman of Wye upsets the drivers who run her down for another reason. She smiles at them. Just before the moment of impact, the ghost turns and smiles pleasantly at the driver. It is a warm, welcoming smile. And it is utterly unnerving.

Kent's most beautiful ghost is seen walking along the lanes outside Wye.

PLUCKLEY

It is difficult to mention the place Pluckley without adding its main claim to fame as 'The most haunted village in England'. If the local stories are anything to go by, it is a reputation that is well deserved. There are so many ghosts here that it is wise to deal with them in some sort of order, and starting at the local pub seems as good a place as any other.

The building now functioning as the Black Horse Inn is over 700 years old in parts, though some of it is much more modern. It was a private house for most of its history, becoming an inn in Victorian times. The ghost here is invisible, but makes its presence strongly felt nonetheless. It is most irritating for the landlord and staff to find that keys, papers or clothes that they have carefully put down in one place are suddenly no longer there. Sometimes the objects turn up in another room or tucked away in a drawer. Such incidents could well be explained as

*The Black Horse Inn at Pluckley,
haunted both inside and out.*

momentary lapses of concentration and, indeed, few people have not had an object go missing in this way. But at the Black Horse these things happen more than is usual. Even more bizarre is the fact that objects may go missing, only to turn up where they were left a day, a week or even a month later. A succession of landlords have put the inexplicable events down to the resident ghost.

Just outside the pub is Dicky Buss's Lane where a schoolmaster committed suicide in the early 19th century. Before taking his life, the man dressed himself in his best frock coat and striped trousers. It is in this elegant outfit that he appears in spectral form.

Not far away, where the Pinnock stream is crossed by a bridge is the site of what was once a watermill. The old building burnt down in 1939, just before war broke out. Standing idly beside the gentle waters is sometimes seen the ghost of a man dressed in a long white smock. It is assumed that this is the miller of the long vanished mill, though why he should return to haunt the site of his old workplace is not entirely clear. Some think he died after his sweetheart left him for another man.

The bridge is also the site of another, and quite horrific haunting. Over a century ago, this bridge was frequented by an old woman who would sit here selling watercress to villagers and passersby. Late one evening the old lady had nodded off to sleep when her claypipe fell from her lips and set fire to her clothing. Her shrieks brought people running to put out the flames, but the poor lady died of her injuries. For some time afterwards the whole scene was repeatedly played out in all its horrific details. In recent years, however, the phantom has been reduced to little more than a red glow seen bobbing about along the bridge at dusk. Few villagers can have been sorry to see this ghost fade away.

Just across the bridge is the aptly named Fright Corner. This place is home to both an impressively large tree and to yet another phantom highwayman. The luckless robber seems to have been one of the more violent practitioners of his profession. He had been out robbing coaches on a nearby main road when he was surprised by a body of armed men resolute on capturing him and taking him to be hanged. Determined not to endure this grim fate, the highwayman put his spurs to his horse and rode hell for leather. He got as far as Pluckley before his horse failed him. Backing up against the tree at Fright Corner, the highwayman held off his attackers until finally stabbed through the chest by a man wielding a heavy cavalry sabre.

Pluckley's parish church of St Nicholas which has two ghosts.

Gruesomely the sword pinned the robber to the tree, supporting the dead body upright until it was taken away for burial. It is this scene that the haunting re-creates. On nights when the moon is full, the shade of the highwayman is seen pinned to the tree by the heavy blade of a sabre. So still and pale is the ghost that some have not noticed it until they are almost upon it. It gives them quite a shock.

The nearby parish church of St Nicholas has two ghosts, both of them women. The older ghost is the phantom of the Wicked Lady Dering, a noted Kent beauty of the 17th century. The exact nature of her alleged wickedness is not recorded, but it is said to have been as impressive as the beauty and charm with which she masked it. When Lady Dering died, her grieving husband laid a single red rose in her hands just before the coffin lid was closed down. The body was then interred in the vault of the Dering Chapel where it lies to this day. The ghost, however, is not restricted to the family chapel but wanders freely around the church and churchyard. The elegant lady still clasps to her breast the single fragrant bloom with which she was interred. Whether or not the strange knocking noise sometimes heard coming from beneath the church floor is connected to Lady Dering is not known.

The other ghost at the church is of a woman in a modern dress of a reddish colour. She has been seen walking among the tombstones, but vanishes with alarming swiftness if approached. She seems to be searching for a particular grave, perhaps her own or perhaps that of a loved one.

The High Street outside the church is the site of the frequent sighting of a carriage and horses which trot along from north to south. Until the 1950s the carriage was often seen and was described as being empty, other than the figure of the tall driver. Another coach, which might be the same vehicle, has been seen two miles further off towards Smarden.

Station Road is home to another haunting resulting from a suicide. This time the ghosts are those of a young couple who walk gently along the lane accompanied by their gambolling little dog. Although most villagers are certain that these two ghosts are connected to a love triangle that ended in suicide, nobody can give any details. Nor is it clear how the ghostly dog is involved. They appear to be quite gentle phantoms, and clearly in love, going about their own business.

Outside of the village itself are the tumbled ruins of old Surrenden Dering House. Along with most of the buildings in the village itself, this was sold off when the Dering Estate was broken up in 1928. It served as a boys' school until 1952 when it was destroyed by fire, leaving the blackened ruins seen today. The house and grounds have long been haunted by a Lady Dering, though this is

The sign that welcomes visitors to the village of Pluckley strangely makes no mention of the many ghosts to haunt the place.

apparently a different lady from that who haunts the church, for no hint of any wickedness attaches to this phantom.

This ghost was so life-like and apparently solid that in the 1930s a friend of one of the schoolmasters became convinced that she was, in fact, a dummy or other trick cooked up by some of the more ingenious boys. When he himself saw the phantom one evening he took the drastic step of firing a revolver over her head and demanding that the supposed tricksters show themselves. When no boys appeared, he shot the phantom itself – though with no obvious effect.

The woods which once stood around the old manor have now been felled, but they are still home to the ghost of an army officer found dead among the trees over 200 years ago. Smart in his red coat and bright buttons, the officer strides out as if on some determined mission, though the secret of what it might be died with him and remains a mystery.

There can be no doubt that Pluckley more than lives up to its reputation as being the most haunted village in England. With its many tales of woe, death and suicide, it would seem that it is not the most pleasant of places to live. But this is far from the truth. The village is a charming and welcoming one where an enjoyable afternoon can be whiled away tracking down the sites of the many hauntings.

SMARDEN

Back in around 1812 the Napoleonic Wars were in full swing. Britain was locked in a ferocious struggle with the military dictatorship of the Emperor of France and his allies. Arthur Wellesley, soon to be the Duke of Wellington, was leading a small but effective British army against the French occupation forces in Portugal and Spain while the Royal Navy cruised the high seas to ensure that the French fleet was kept bottled up in port.

In those days it was customary for soldiers and sailors to be rewarded with prize money for anything they captured that would be of use to the war effort. Artillery, ammunition, ships, stores and provisions were all purchased by the government and the prize money was shared out among the men involved in the capture. Some men could make their fortunes in this way and those who resisted the temptations of gambling, drinking and womanising could end their service in the armed forces with a useful nest egg for their retirement.

One such soldier returning from the wars with a full purse and plans to buy a farm or tavern stopped off at the Chequers in Smarden on his way home. He had the misfortune to fall in with a 17 year old girl who was far

The Chequers Inn at Smarden, the haunted bedroom is that which overlooks this courtyard at the rear of the pub.

prettier than she was honest. The girl plied the man with drink and with flattering attentions. When the soldier retired to bed in Room 6, the girl gave him time to fall asleep, then crept up to rob him. The soldier wakened and the girl stabbed him in the ensuing struggle. The poor man died and the girl fled.

It is this murdered soldier who returns to the Chequers. He moves objects about, taking a particular delight in hiding kitchen utensils. He will place cutlery where it does not belong or put it out for use when it should be tidied away. He will bring plates and pans into the pub that no member of staff has ever seen before, and then take them away again a few days later. He is most active upstairs after dark.

Charlie, the landlord in 2003, makes a great feature of his fine cooking and sources all food locally. He also caters to the bed and breakfast market, renting out several rooms including the haunted Room 6. 'It's a funny thing,' said Charlie, 'but the ghost never bothers anyone sleeping in Room 6. But when that room is empty he can get very active indeed. One chap we had staying here went so far as to complain about the noise made by the man in the room next to his walking around late at night. The room next to his was Room 6, but there was nobody in it. It was just our ghost. Of course, I've had several people come here and ask to see the haunted room. So long as we have nobody staying in it, I am happy to show people up. After all, they usually stop for a bite to eat. Our ghost is good for business.'

OXNEY BOTTOM

The tiny area known as Oxney Bottom between Dover and Deal is small enough to be completely unnoticed by modern humans as they hurry about their business. But the phantom world is rather more interested in this area, making it, just possibly, the scariest place in England.

Even on a bright, sunny day Oxney Bottom can be a bit unnerving. The main road dips down into a patch of dense woodland which casts a disconcerting darkness over the road. It then bends sharply before climbing back out into the sunlight. This site was once a village, a thriving community

HAUNTED PLACES OF KENT

of Kent farmers and their families. The village was torn apart by religious rioting during the Reformation and the parish church was subjected to a particularly ruthless bout of iconoclastic violence.

By 1700 the village had been abandoned and the church had become a barn connected to the nearby mansion of Oxney Court, home of the Roffey family. Today both house and church stand in ruins, uncared for by anyone and in danger of final collapse. It is this neglected, abandoned place that attracts the phantoms and a strange sense of dread.

The best known of the Oxney ghosts is the Grey Lady who lurks beside the road where it takes its sharp turn. This lady, whoever she may be, will appear quite suddenly beside the road just as a car approaches and step out as if to cross. More than one driver has slammed on his brakes desperately trying to avoid an accident. During the 1960s there were several crashes here caused by motorists swerving to avoid the phantom. Fortunately nobody was seriously injured.

In the 1950s a bus stopped here one evening to allow on board what the driver took to be an old lady flagging him down, but there was nobody there. The same Grey Lady was seen as recently as the spring of 2003 by a man from Richborough. Knowing the stories about the ghost, the man stopped his car and got out to investigate, but the apparition had disappeared.

Spooky as the appearance of the Grey Lady may be, she is nothing compared to the 'something' that lurks around the ruined church. Local gossip has it that a child once fell down an abandoned well here and was killed. Be that as it may, many people have come away from the church wishing they had not visited. 'I encountered a strange feeling of being watched by something,' recalled one visitor to the ruin in the 1990s. 'Whatever it was did not like my being there. I swear I felt something, which was when I fled.'

'A friend and I went to investigate the stories', reported a more courageous individual, 'and we took a camcorder. My friend went into the church to set up the camera while I had a look around outside. A few minutes later my friend came running out to me and insisted we left, at once. All he said was that we were not welcome there and had to leave.'

When the author was investigating this place in September 2003 he spoke to the landlord of a local pub to ask for information. 'I wouldn't go there, if I was you', came the response. 'Not after dark. Not on foot. It is a real strange place.'

DOVER

As ghosts go, few fit the popular cliché of a spooky phantom better than the notorious headless drummer of Dover Castle. The unfortunate boy has patrolled the battlements for two centuries, and looks set to march on for many years to come. But he is not the only phantom at Dover or, by some centuries, the oldest.

It is, however, the drummer boy which is the best known of Dover's ghosts. The luckless lad was part of the garrison here during the long summer of 1805. The French Emperor Napoleon had a vast army camped around Boulogne, just on the other side of the Channel. On clear days the French scouts on the opposite coast were visible from the ramparts of Dover Castle. All Napoleon needed was control of the sea and he would use this coastal army to conquer Britain. Day after day the scouts on both sides of the Channel scanned the western horizon for signs of the French fleet coming from Toulon and Brest. The French ships never came, however, because the Royal Navy, led by Admiral Nelson, held them off and finally defeated them at the Battle of Trafalgar in the October.

Although the invasion never came, it was a real possibility during the summer months. Even more likely were French coastal raids to test possible invasion landing sites or to damage coastal defences. Such raids were most likely on moonless nights, and it was to guard against such attacks that the drummer boy was set to patrol the battlements of Dover Castle. All British boats and ships were ordered to stay in port on such nights, so any craft seen moving had to be French.

One dark night, the drummer boy was put on duty and given orders to beat the alert as loud as he could the instant he saw anything. When the watch changed, his battered and decapitated body was found crumpled at the foot of

Dover Castle, home to a number of phantoms and ghosts.

the castle walls. Nobody was ever caught for the crime. It was assumed he had witnessed a crime and been silenced by the ruthless crooks.

Before long the boy returned. His headless phantom strode up and down the battlements, his immaculate drum hanging loosely by his side. He appears only at night, when the moon is dark. It seems he is determined to continue forever the patrol cut short so savagely back on that summer's night in 1805.

Dover Castle has other ghosts. The ground floor of the keep is the haunt of a richly dressed gentleman in 17th century outfit. Equipped with knee-high riding boots and swathed in a richly purple cloak this dashing figure is topped off by a wide-brimmed hat adorned with a dramatic plume. Known simply as 'the cavalier' this ghost has the habit of walking through doorways and promptly vanishing into thin air. It can be most unnerving, but he does not cause any real trouble.

Equally dramatic in appearance is 'the lady in red' who walks about on an upper floor of the keep. She is seen most often near the staircase. Like the cavalier, this phantom is harmless enough. She simply stands and looks about her before gently fading from view.

The King's Bedroom is the centre of an altogether more disturbing haunting. Many people cannot bear to be in the room. One visitor in May 2003 entered the chamber, only to turn and dash straight back out again. 'There was this most horrid feeling,' she explained afterwards. 'It was like a man was in there causing torment and death. I couldn't stand it a moment longer.' Such events are not uncommon, but a phantom has been seen only once. This was the disturbing apparition of a man's legs and lower body striding across the room. The member of staff who saw the half figure was so startled that, not surprisingly, she took some time to recover. Who, or what, lurks here is unknown.

Within the walls of the medieval Dover Castle stands the rugged tower which is all that remains of the Roman fortifications. This octagonal tower was built as a lighthouse to guide Roman ships into the harbour.

In the 10th century it was converted into a bell tower for a church dedicated to St Mary, but continued to serve as a landmark to mariners. It is beside this tower that a figure in white has been seen to walk. Some claim this is a phantom Roman dressed in a toga, but the descriptions of the apparition are generally pretty vague.

In the rocks, deep beneath the Castle, are a series of tunnels which are thought to date back to Roman times. Every generation that has occupied this site since the Romans built their lighthouse has added to the tunnels. Most recently the caverns and passages were occupied by the armed forces during World War II. During 1940 the port and town came under such sustained and heavy attack by the Luftwaffe that the Dover area became known as Hellfire Corner. And that was before the Germans brought up long range artillery to bombard the town from fields around Calais.

Faced by such a rain of bombs and shells, the service personnel stationed in Dover retreated underground. The tunnels became a complex of offices, store rooms, command centres and even a fully-equipped hospital. It is the area that was once the hospital that seems to be the centre of the hauntings in this subterranean complex. The ghosts seen most often is that of a soldier in 1940s

The gates to Dover's Connaught Park, where one of Kent's most bizarre phantoms has been seen.

khaki uniform. He is said to be fairly short and stocky, but no witness can give a clear description of his face. He walks purposefully along the corridors and through doors, but quite what his mission might be nobody knows. Perhaps he is the phantom of one of those injured in the incessant bombing raids of 1940 when, once again, Dover braced itself for a foreign invasion that never came.

A second ghost in the tunnels is seen much less often. This is of a nurse who brushes her hair or straightens her uniform. Perhaps she is getting ready to go on duty. Like the soldier, she has a habit of passing out of sight through a door behind a piece of furniture and so vanishing completely.

Thus far the ghosts of Dover have been a fairly routine bunch as phantoms go. Headless drummers, phantom cavaliers and a lady in red are not unknown elsewhere. But the ghost that terrifies people in Connaught Park is unique to Dover. This phantom appears dramatically around dusk, looming up out of the gloom like some dreadful monster, which is a fairly accurate description.

Shaped much like a man this ghost towers seven feet tall. Its head is grotesque to say the least. One witness described the apparition as having a dog's head, another that it has a long beak. The monstrously deformed head of this spectre causes alarm and fright, before the ghost vanishes as suddenly as it appeared. 'Strange stuff', as one local put it.

SALTWOOD

The apparently inoffensive little village of Saltwood is a veritable magnet for the supernatural. If it cannot rival the more famous Pluckley for sheer numbers of ghosts, it certainly has the edge when it comes to oddness. More than one witness has used the word 'bizarre' when talking about Saltwood.

The road from Saltwood village to the railway station at Sanding is haunted by a nocturnal ghost which, at first sight, seems to be nothing at all unusual. To begin with the phantom appears as a small light which bobs about (much like the tragic actor in the Margate theatre). Those who have seen it say it looks like a torch or old-style lantern being carried along. This is not at all an unlikely occurrence given the lack of street lighting along this rural road. When the light gets closer it reveals itself to be a lantern being carried by a tall, rather elderly man. The man walks forward hesitantly, as if using the lantern to search for something in the roadway. He is the ghost of a local farmer who lived here in the 19th century and was famed for his eccentric behaviour. Nightly rambles to search the roads and paths were typical, though he never told anyone what he was looking for and would hurry off if he saw anyone watching him.

He has not changed on becoming a ghost. Once the phantom gets close to a living person he hurriedly shuffles off and the light is quickly extinguished.

The road near Brockhill School has a pair of phantoms, though some suspect that they might be one and the same. The most often seen spectre is that of a woman taking her dog for a walk. The lady is dressed in sensible tweeds of around the 1930s and the dog scampers along quite happily. Apart from the slightly old-fashioned looks of the lady's clothes there is nothing to mark the pair out from a living lady and dog. There is, however, something indefinably odd about the pair. It is not entirely certain what it is that is unusual, but those who have seen them all agree that they are strange. It is said to be like looking at a painting in which the perspective is slightly askew. Everything is there and in its right place, but somehow the picture is just 'wrong'.

The second ghost of the Brockhill area is another lady, though this one does not seem to be accompanied by a pet. She appears quite suddenly standing beside the road, then steps out into the carriageway as if to cross the road. Barely halfway across the road she suddenly vanishes. The lady is not in view long enough for anyone to give a good description of her, but again there is agreement that there is something odd about the lady, in addition to her sudden appearance and disappearance of course.

The stream that runs through Saltwood has the ominous name of Slaybrook. Local legend has it that the name commemorates an ancient battle which was so fierce that the stream ran red with blood for a full week after the struggle took place. As at so many places in Kent, the fight is ascribed to the Romans and the Celts. This time, however, the supposed battle is not said to have taken place during the invasion campaign, but some years later.

It is said that the Celts of Saltwood were adept at waylaying and robbing lone travellers using the Roman road to Canterbury. Hardly surprisingly the Romans decided to put an end to the raids. A force of legionaries was marched into Saltwood where they met resistance from the errant tribesmen. The Romans were victorious, wiping out the nest of robbers and then going too far in slaughtering the women and children as well as the guilty men.

It is said that the Roman centurion who ordered the massacre later repented of his deeds and returns to the scene of his crime to weep over the souls of the butchered innocents. The guilt-ridden spirit of the Roman appears on chill autumn evenings when the clammy air over the stream forms into soft tendrils of white mist. One patch of mist will gradually thicken and swirl as if stirred by some invisible force. Slowly the mist assumes the shape of an armoured man, carrying a square shield and wearing a helmet with a crest. Gradually the figure emerges from the mist as a white figure more solid than the surrounding vapour, but still strangely insubstantial. He stops beside the banks of the stream, bends his head in remorse and weeps. Then the figure slowly disperses and drifts away until all that is left is the rolling mist of a still autumn evening. It is, apparently, a distinctly chilling performance to watch.

Perhaps the oddest of the ghosts of Saltwood is the so-called Mothman. This bizarre apparition was seen most clearly on the night of 16 November 1963 when four teenagers were walking down the Sanding road after dark. As they passed the wood, they saw lights behind the trees, but paid them little attention. As they moved away from the trees one of the teenagers looked across the open fields and saw a figure approaching at a shambling run. There was something odd about the figure, so the teenager pointed it out to his companions.

One of the boys, John, described what happened next to a local newspaper. 'There was a silhouette which fell down heavily. Then got up. It was very black and about the size of a man, but it had no head. It appeared to have wings on either side of the body – like a bat. It came towards us, stumbling as it came. We did not wait to find out what it was, but ran.'

Soon after the incident made the local press, others were coming forward to say that they had seen something similar in the area but had kept quiet for fear of ridicule. The strange headless giant bat became something of a local wonder, but sightings soon tailed off and the story died down. Then, in 1966, a very similar creature was seen in the USA. This time the winged monster was identified as being part man, part moth and became famous as 'the Mothman'. It was linked to UFOs and so the Saltwood apparition has become part of UFO culture, featuring in many books and articles on the subject.

APPLEDORE

The ghosts who wander boisterously around Appledore are those of four unfortunate Canadian soldiers who lived here for a few weeks in 1942. They left this charming place to find death in France.

By 1942 the war against Hitler's Germany had taken a new turn. The dark days when invasion threatened Britain were gone. The German army and Luftwaffe were deeply engaged in the war against Russia, a war which was not going well for Hitler. Britain and her allies were now flying bombing raids over Germany and commandos raided the enemy-occupied coasts of France and the Low Countries. Sooner or later, it was hoped, it would be possible to mount a full scale invasion across the Channel and drive the Germans out of France.

The key problem with such an invasion, the military planners believed, was not so much getting the men ashore as keeping them supplied with food and ammunition once they got there. What was needed was a port, but many doubted that it would be possible to capture a port before the defending Germans had time to sabotage all the dock facilities. It was decided to launch a raid on the port of Dieppe in August 1942 to test how quickly the docks and equipment could be captured. Lord Louis Mountbatten was put in charge of a strong naval task force, three full commando units and the 2nd Canadian Division.

In preparation for the Dieppe Raid, the Canadians were moved to Kent where they were put through training exercises for landing on beaches and practised capturing key buildings in Dieppe using mock-ups. And so the four Canadian soldiers were billeted in Appledore in a small house just off the High Street. Along with their fellows, the four became popular if boisterous guests of the town. Their good humour, jokes and ribaldry quickly became famous.

In August they left to take part in the ill-fated raid. It was a fiasco. British intelligence about the German defences turned out to be faulty, which meant the naval bombardment left several artillery and machine gun emplacements intact. One part of the task force ran into a German patrol boat in the Channel, so that the element of surprise was lost. Even worse, the Germans had their new Focke Wulf 190 fighter in the area in large numbers. It was the first time the RAF had encountered the FW190 and they were quickly cleared from the skies. In all 3,400 Canadians, 250 commandos and 150 RAF men were killed or captured. More than half the force had been lost.

The military planners claimed that they had learnt valuable lessons about landing on a defended coast line. Those lessons were put into practice on D-Day in 1944 when the Allies eventually did invade German-occupied France.

That was, however, little consolation to the thousands of Canadian casualties whose bodies were left floating on the sea off Dieppe. Among them were the four soldiers who had made Appledore their second home.

It was not long before the four men came back to the Kent town. This was the last place on earth where they had enjoyed themselves, so perhaps this is why they return so frequently. They stroll around the streets, laughing and joking with each other in evident enjoyment. It is as if nothing has changed for them since those long summer evenings of 1942 before they went to their deaths in Dieppe.

DYMCHURCH

The charming little town of Dymchurch stands on the edge of Romney Marsh. Its history is peopled by smugglers, fishermen and farmers as is that of every other town and village around this area. And at the heart of all the activity is the Ship Inn which stands on the High Street.

The pub dates back to the 16th century and the old part of the building is riddled with hidden cupboards and at least one secret passage. This was discovered in 1988 when the wallpaper in the lounge was stripped to reveal a hatch. Behind the hatch was a tiny room from which ran a passage that snaked around inside the thick walls. No doubt it was of great use to the smugglers attempting to evade the revenue men. Many visitors are puzzled by the layout of the pub. It has its back facing the High Street and its front facing the sea wall. This is because the original main road ran along the old sea wall. In 1886 the sea wall was improved and a new road built along the backs of the various buildings.

The ghost of the Ship is not, so far as we know, connected to smuggling. Andy Sharp, the 'guv'nor' of the Ship, as he calls himself, knows all about the phantom.

'One evening when I had gone to bed, I was just falling asleep when I heard a creaking of floorboards right outside my bedroom door. My bedroom is situated in the attic of the building, facing the Channel. I assumed it was my eldest daughter getting up to go to the toilet, but I listened and realised that

One of several secret rooms hidden in the Ship Inn at Dymchurch which were probably used by smugglers to hide their illegal imports.

the noise was not going away. It sounded like someone was out there walking around in a circle because each floorboard creaked a bit differently. I stayed in bed until I worked up the courage to see what it was. As I opened the door the noise stopped. Nothing was there. To this day I have not heard the same noise again. My room is above one of the bed and breakfast rooms we use for letting out and some have said that, this being an old building, people moving downstairs were causing the floorboards on our level to creak. A good theory, but we did not have any guests that particular evening.

'A few weeks back I had a couple of mediums stop here for a drink. They told me that they had spoken to our lady. They said she was very happy here.'

So who is this walking ghost? The story that accompanies the haunting is that many generations ago a maid at the Ship was jilted by her lover shortly before their wedding day. The distraught girl ran home and committed suicide in her room in the attic. Since then she has been heard walking around upstairs and, sometimes, has been seen on the upper floors. She is dressed in a long grey dress which reaches to the floor.

'Don't worry about her,' was the guv'nor's advice. 'She appears friendly.'

LYDD

G iven the history of this town in Romney Marsh it might be thought that a smuggler would be the appropriate phantom to lurk here. Instead, it is a rather charming and playful spectral cat which has been noticed at the George Hotel. Since the 1970s people staying there have reported that as soon as they switch off their lights at night they feel a cat jump up onto their bed and walk about with dainty steps. Thinking that a resident cat has been lurking under the bed, they switch the light back on. There is, however, no cat to be seen.

ROMNEY MARSH

I f there is one fictional character who can be said to encapsulate the atmosphere of the misty landscape and equally misty past of wild Romney Marsh, apart from Dickens's Magwitch, it is Doctor Syn. This 18th century rector, a literary creation of local writer Russell Thorndyke, had a secret nocturnal life as the dashing leader of a gang of smugglers who brought brandy, lace and other luxuries into England illegally over the marsh. He fell in love with the daughter of a local squire and launched into a famous romance. These days the life of Doctor Syn is celebrated in local fetes and festivals. The main event is held every two years when the activities are co-ordinated into the appropriately named 'Days of Syn'.

One real smuggler was less fortunate than the fictional Doctor Syn. He ended his days on a gibbet just outside the village of Brookland after being caught by the revenue men. After his body had been left to rot for some weeks, his remains were cut down and buried by the roadside. Ever since then he has returned to pace restlessly around the site of the now-vanished gibbet.

Around Old Romney a rather more dramatic haunting takes place, usually in mid-afternoon. The customary quiet of Romney Marsh is disturbed by the throbbing roar of approaching aircraft engines. These are not jet engines, but the piston engines that power propeller driven aircraft. The noise gets louder and more insistent, though no aircraft can be seen anywhere in the sky. Suddenly the engines take on a more urgent and dramatic tone which turns into a terrifying scream, as the aircraft dives down at great speed. Clearly it is in trouble if the shriek of tortured metal and the rising howl of the engines is anything to go by. As the volume of noise reaches a climax of ear-bursting intensity it suddenly stops and silence returns. It is as if nothing has happened.

Locals claim that this noisy performance is given by the ghost of a German bomber shot down over Romney Marsh during the Battle of Britain in 1940. No wreckage has ever been found around Old Romney, but the marsh is a deep place and could easily swallow the wreckage of an aircraft, especially if it hit the ground fast enough to bury itself in the deep, soft earth.

· Index ·

HAUNTED PLACES OF KENT